Timberdoodle
TINY TOTS

Curriculum Handbook

2024-2025

We're So Glad You Are Here

Congratulations on choosing to homeschool this year! Whether this is your first year as a teacher or your tenth, we're confident you'll find that there is very little that compares to watching your child's learning take off. We suspect you'll look back at this year as one that shaped your relationship with your child and made you closer than ever.

On Your Mark, Get Set, Go!

Preparing for your first school day is very easy. Peruse this guide, customize your schedule, browse the introductions in your books, and you will be ready to go.

We Are Here to Help

We would love to assist you if questions come up, so please don't hesitate to contact us with any questions, comments, or concerns. Whether you contact us by phone, email, or live online chat, you will get a real person who is eager to serve you and your family.

You Will Love This!

This year you and your student will learn more than you hoped while having a blast. Ready? Have an absolutely amazing year!

Schedule Customizer

Your 2024-2025 Tiny Tots Curriculum Kit includes access to our Schedule Customizer, where you can not only plan out your school weeks but also tweak the checklist to include exactly what you want on your schedule. To get started, just visit the scheduling website:

schedule.timberdoodle.com

If you ordered online under the same email address as your Schedule Customizer account, your kit is preloaded and ready to schedule now! If not, use your activation code + order number to gain access now. (See page 10 for complete activation information.)

Your Timberdoodle Activation Code:

79MH36L9SHSP

You'll also need your order number. If you ordered from a school district or don't have it handy, call, email, or chat with us, and we will be happy to look it up for you.

Get Support

Are you looking for a place to hang out online with like-minded homeschoolers? Do you wonder how someone else handled a particular science kit? Or do you wish you could encourage someone who is just getting started this year? Join one or more of our online groups.

Timberdoodlers of all ages:

https://www.facebook.com/groups/Timberdoodle

Timberdoodlers with students ages 0 to K:

https://www.facebook.com/groups/EarlyTimberdoodle

Timberdoodlers using nonreligious kits:

https://www.facebook.com/groups/SecularTimberdoodle

Timberdoodle.com | 800-478-0672

Contents

Introductory Matters

5	Meet Your Handbook
6	You are Going to Love This!
8	Planning Your Year
10	Meet Your Online Schedule Customizer
14	Introducing The Reading Challenge
18	Tiny Tots Overview
20	Your Annual Planner
22	Sample Weekly Checklists

Weekly Checklists Age-by-Age

27	Planning By Developmental Age
28	Newborn through 3 Months
34	4-6 Months
40	7-9 Months
46	10-12 Months
52	13-16 Months
58	17-20 Months
64	21-24 Months

Item-by-Item Introductions

71	Active Baby, Healthy Brain
73	Language Arts
86	Mathematics
88	STEM Learning
98	Emotional Intelligence
106	Motor Skills
111	Sensory Skills

Articles and Resources

117	From Our Family to Yours
118	Homeschooling Your Baby: Learning Styles
120	Homeschooling Your Baby: The Ideal Environment
122	Get Into a Routine You Love
124	Our Family's Routine
126	9 Tips for Homeschooling with a Toddler
128	Can We Talk about Obedience?
130	10 Reasons to Stop Schoolwork and Go Build Something!
132	9 Tips for Homeschooling Gifted Children
134	11 Thoughts for Homeschooling Struggling Children
136	Convergent & Divergent Thinking
138	Sensory Bins
140	Workbooks as Blank Walls
142	I Need a Homeschool Group, Right?

The Reading Challenge

145	Reading Challenge Questions & Answers
150	Tracking Your Reading Challenge
152	36 Weeks of Reading Challenges
224	Book Awards & Party

When You're Done Here

227	Your Top 4 FAQ about Next Year
228	Doodle Dollar Reward Points

Introductory Matters

Meet Your Handbook

Simple Is Better

1. The Planning

First up are all the details on planning your year, including your annual planner and sample weekly checklists, which are the absolute backbones of Timberdoodle's curriculum kits. More on those in a moment.

2. Let's Talk about Your Baby

We then take a few pages to discuss things you'll target at different ages and stages of development. We share case studies and show how to customize your plan to meet your child's needs rather than using a one-size-fits-all approach.

3. Item-by-Item Introductions

We include short bios of each item in your kit, ideal for refreshing your memory on why each is included or explaining exactly what your little one will be learning this year. This is where we've tucked in teaching tips to make this year easy and amazing for both of you.

4. Articles and Resources

In this section you'll find our favorite articles and tidbits gathered over 35 years of homeschool experience.

5. Reading Challenge

Last but not least is the reading challenge—a reading log designed to help your child read a huge variety of books this year. We include hundreds of book ideas to give you a head start. While it may seem surprising to do a reading challenge with someone this tiny, just think about the variety of literature you'll encounter while soaking up snuggles and beautiful moments with your child. We include dozens of book ideas to give you a head start.

All the Details Included

This Timberdoodle curriculum kit is available in three different levels. The Infant Kit features items most utilized by ages 0–12 months. The Toddler Kit includes the items most used for 12– through 24-month-olds. The Tiny Tots Birth to 2 Kit includes all the components for 0–24 months. In this guide, you'll find an overview and tips for each of the items included in the Tiny Tots Birth to 2 Curriculum Kit. If you purchased an Infant or Toddler Kit, or if you customized your kit, you chose not to receive every item. You'll only need to familiarize yourself with the products which were included in your kit.

Don't Panic—You Didn't Order Too Much Stuff!

We have yet to meet a homeschooler who doesn't have other irons in the fire. From homesteading or running a business to swimming lessons or doctor appointments, your weeks are not dull. As you unpack your box, you may be wondering how you'll fit it all in. We'll go in-depth on schedules momentarily, but for now, know that most of the items in your kit feature short lessons, and not all of them should be done every day or even every week. Your checklist (aka the weekly to-do list) is going to make this incredibly manageable. Really!

You are Going to Love This!

Getting Started, Siblings, and More

Newborn to 24 months is a huge developmental range to cover in a single curriculum set, especially considering how much your child changes and grows during this time.

For this kit we have included our most invaluable, unusual, and versatile materials, designed to grow with your baby. Once he has mastered these tools, he is ready for the preschool set, even if he isn't yet over 24 months.

By the same token, some two-year-olds will be best served by spending more time with these tools, so don't rush your toddler into preschool either!

Planning

Your goal is to pace your baby so that he is constantly learning but not overwhelmed. Our family likes to use a weekly check-off sheet so that nothing gets lost in the shuffle. Print it from the online schedule customizer so that you can modify it for your child, or photocopy the appropriate pages in this guide.

What Is the Goal?

We aren't interested in producing the smartest baby in the world just to prove we can. Instead, our goal is to give you tools and ideas of things to do with your baby that stimulate him mentally and physically and, even more importantly, to help you develop a deeper relationship with your child while maximizing his strengths and minimizing his weaknesses.

Since your baby is wired to learn, the question is not whether you will teach him but what you will teach and how deliberately you will go about it.

Character First

Another thing to keep in mind is that more than educating your baby, you are teaching this little one how to learn. Build his attention span little by little. Encourage perseverance when he wants to fling the pieces across the floor. Feed his curiosity for all things moving. Reward hard work, encourage language development, and expect obedience as he matures.

These are more than just life skills—they are part of character development, and as such they are much more important than any academic skill.

Reading Second

Make it your goal to spend time reading with your baby every day. We have included several books in your kit to get you started, but please don't think that they are truly enough. Supplement them with books from your library or your family's own collection.

Regardless of what you choose to read, make it part of your daily routine to sit down and read together. Not only does this develop his own appetite for reading, but it is also an incredible tool for building vocabulary and budding language skills.

Siblings

If your baby is blessed with older siblings, keep them involved in his education. Not only will he have more opportunities to learn, but his siblings will learn the invaluable skill of teaching. We suggest going over the weekly chart and highlighting the things you'd like them to do. For instance, everything highlighted yellow is for big brother to do, and the ones in green are reserved for big sister. Then let them check the work off as they go. Baby will love it, the siblings will be delighted with their accomplishments, and you just might get a moment to plan tonight's menu!

Photo: The McClures Family in the Carolinas

Planning Your Year

How To Use Timberdoodle's Planners, Setting Up Your First Week, and More

Photo: The H. Family in Mississippi

Make This Work for You

In all the chaos of caring for and feeding a tiny one, we find ourselves asking: Did we do the puzzle twice this week, or was it last week? When was the last time baby actually had tummy time? To make your life easier, we've included simple weekly checklists. You'll be able to see at a glance that you really haven't tackled sensory play yet this week, but you've done motor skills three times already. As always, capitalize on what interests you and your baby, and don't be tied to a script. But we still think you'll find the at-a-glance ideas to be both helpful and freeing.

Designed for Maximum Flexibility

No two families are identical, so don't expect your pace or daily school time to be either. Are you off to the dentist this week? You won't fall behind by taking a day off. Or perhaps you'd like to save the most travel-friendly tools for your big trip this weekend. That's not a problem!

Active Baby, Healthy Brain

If you can do only one part of this kit, please make it this book. It covers so much! To make implementing it easier, we've added Active Baby checklists in the age-by-age sections.

Our 27 Babies

In addition to the five original Timberdoodlers (now grown) and the four grandchildren that have been added by birth, in over seven years of foster care we've also welcomed into our home 23 tiny ones (so far) who were under the age of two. From the newborn just discharged from the hospital to the 22-month-old who needed a safe place for a day, each little one has taught us much. The biggest lesson? Each child is SO different! Along with your starter schedules, we'll be including notes with possible scenarios where you'd want to adjust your plans to boost your child's development. (Just FYI, we won't be using the real names or precise scenarios that we've encountered—even if we have learned a ton from "our" precious ones!)

We Aren't Going to Talk about This

Your app or parenting book will tell you how many times a day to expect to feed your tiny one, how to swaddle him, and when to anticipate developmental milestones. We're going to leave that for the experts and focus on our area of expertise—connecting with your child while you grow his brain.

A Little Every Day or All at Once?

At this age, you'll want to spread out topics throughout the week as much as possible. For instance, it will be better for your baby's brain to read together multiple times a week instead of one super-long reading session. Use common sense, though—if you're on a reading roll, don't stop just because you ran out of checkboxes on your list!

Week 1 Hints

As you get started this year, realize that you are just getting your sea legs. Expect your routine to take a little longer and be a little less smooth than it will be by the end of the month. As you get your feet under you, you will discover the rhythm that works best for you! If you don't know where to begin each day, why not try starting with something from *Active Baby, Healthy Brain*? It will get your child's brain in gear and set a great tone for the rest of the day.

Meet Your Online Schedule Customizer
Getting the Most Out of Your Planner

Newest Feature

Among the many behind-the-scenes improvements already completed and the bigger updates scheduled for spring, there is one new feature on the site that you'll want to know about now: You can now see at a glance which things you skipped in previous weeks. This will make catching up even easier!

Use the Customizer

Beginning on page 22, you'll find sample weekly checklists for Infant, Toddler, and Tiny Tots (everything) kits. Before you photocopy 36 of them, though, take a moment to check out the online Schedule Customizer that came free with your kit. You can easily adjust your days and weeks of school and tweak the checklist to include exactly what you want. Plus, you'll be able to print your weekly checklists directly from the Schedule Customizer and even log your progress!

First Time?

You'll need to activate your account for the Schedule Customizer to get started. If you ordered from our website, head directly to schedule.timberdoodle.com and log in. Your activated kit will be waiting for you!

If you ordered through a school district or need to activate a different email address, click the button in the middle of the page to submit your activation code from the inside front page of this handbook + your order number and start scheduling!

Photo: The Chiavarios Family in the Midwest

Before you get started, you'll want to know 3 things:

1. How Many Weeks Will You Do School?

A standard school year is 36 weeks plus breaks. Some families prefer to have the same number of checklists for baby as they do for the older siblings. Others will prefer to keep baby's activities going all year, even when the rest of the crew is on break.

2. When Do You Want to Start?

Any day is fair game! You may want to match your local school district, but you don't have to.

3. What Breaks Do You Want?

Thanksgiving, Christmas, winter break, spring break…you could also add weeks off for travel, visiting grandparents, or…

If you are using the weekly checklist, you typically don't need to take the time to enter a single-day break since most families prefer to work a little harder on the other days that week and not lose their stride. But if you're using the daily schedule, or if it's easier for you, feel free to add in partial-week breaks too!

Check Your End Date

A standard school schedule is often 40 weeks long, with 36 weeks of schoolwork + 4 weeks of breaks.

What Days Do You Want to Do School?

If you are using a weekly schedule only, don't worry about this setting! But if you prefer a daily checklist, this is the place to set a 4-day week or move all school from Wednesday to Saturday.

Choose Your Items

Now just pop that data into the Schedule Customizer and proceed to the subject-by-subject review. Under each subject, you'll see your kit's items loaded by default, and you'll also find options to add in items you already had on hand, add custom courses, change the subject color, etc.

Edit Items

If you're opting for the daily scheduler, you have some helpful fine-tuning options. Just click "Edit" on any particular course to select which days of the week the course will appear. This lets you do things like schedule history only on Wednesday because that is co-op day. Or you could schedule science only on Tuesday/Thursday and STEM on Monday/Friday so that science and STEM are never on the same day.

Pro Tip

You can also opt to exclude an item from certain weeks. This is useful if you already know that you want to save Playmobil Community for May so that you can bring it with you to visit Grandma or if you don't want to break out the Ditty Bird books until after Christmas since you've set them aside as a gift.

Front-Load vs. Back-Load

While this is unlikely to be a setting you use much this year with a tiny tot, I suspect you'll still want to know what it does! This setting lets you manually tell the Schedule Customizer what to do with lessons that don't fit neatly into the schedule. E.g., if you have 40 lessons to complete over 36 weeks of school, would you prefer to do the 4 extra lessons over the first 4 weeks of school, the last 4 weeks of school, or spread evenly throughout?

Each will default to "spread evenly," but there are 2 cases where it can be helpful to change it. If it is a course that increases in difficulty as your child progresses (e.g., a Smart Game), then it can make sense to front-load so that he doubles up on the easiest possible lessons. Or if it is an item that builds on other courses (e.g., Daily 6-Trait Writing's 25-week course), then back-loading can make the most sense so that your child has completed as much of the other introductory material as possible before beginning.

Add Custom Courses

Your course list is limited only by your imagination. Perhaps your friend created a custom curriculum you want to include, your family band practices weekly, or you need to include ballet since that's P.E. this year. You can add these by using "Add Course" at the end of the subject-by-subject review.

Schedule Summary

Look over your schedule summary and make sure that everything is the way you want it, then click "Save & Continue." Congratulations—your schedule is complete!

Go to Your Dashboard

Click "Checklist" to print your checklist or log your progress. More about that in a moment.

Make More Lists

If you have 1 student and 1 teacher, feel free to buzz past this idea. But if you have an extra teacher—perhaps your spouse, a grandparent, or even an older sibling—then this may simplify your life! Instead of putting all of your child's work on a single list, you could put only the subjects you will teach on your list and the remaining subjects on "Grandma's list" for her ease.

If you have twins or multiple students at the same grade level, you can also make multiple lists to best meet each student's needs.

Print Your Lists

From the checklist section you can choose to log your progress on the screen or print your checklists. (We prefer a printed checklist for ease of reference, but some of you may find electronic tracking easier. To print, click "Schedule Overview," then set your view options and either download or print your lists.

Here are a few settings you may tweak:

1. Weekly or Daily?

As we discussed already, we generally prefer a weekly schedule for the simple reason that our weeks are rarely without some anomaly. Off to the dentist Tuesday? You won't fall behind by taking a day off. Or perhaps you have Friday Robotics Camp for a couple of weeks and need to get all the week's work done over 4 days instead of 5. No problem! This approach also teaches time-management skills. (See the article on independent learning at the back of this handbook.)

However, we've heard from many of you that having a daily schedule, especially for the first month, is a real lifesaver. The daily option of the Schedule Customizer is programmed to split up the work as evenly as possible over the week, with the beginning of the week having any extra pages or lessons. (We all know that end-of-the-week doldrums are a real thing!)

2. Show Unit Range?

This feature sounds very data-y and not super helpful, but we think you just might love it. Instead of saying that you need to do 7 pages of thinking skills this week, check this box to have it remind you that you're on pages 50–56 this week. If you prefer extreme flexibility, leave this box unchecked. But if you're afraid of falling behind without knowing it, this box will be your hero.

3. Large-Font Edition

Want a large-font option? Just check the box. If you don't like how it looks, you can always come back and uncheck it.

That's It!

Click "Download" or "Print," and you'll be ready to get started in moments! We've heard from a number of you that you prefer to print out your entire year's worth of schedules and spiral bind them at the local print shop. This is a brilliant idea, but we suggest using the checklists for a few weeks first just to make sure you've fine-tuned it as you wish so that you can avoid doing that more than once!

Log Your Progress Online

You now have the ability to log your work as you go. Click "Progress" and log what you've done. As you complete portions, you'll see your progress bars fill in, showing a more tangible representation of your progress this year.

Introducing the Reading Challenge

This Year's Theme: At Home

Photo: The Wahlbrink Family in Arizona

The Reading Challenge for kids will get you and your child reading a broader variety of books this year while covering essential topics.

Your reading challenge introduces 36 different weekly topics to explore together. Choose a book off your library shelf and check off the subject, or go deep with multiple books and activities. Do whatever works for you this week, flexing for at-home weeks with more time to fill and on-the-go weeks that need no extra activities.

At this grade level, your child will read some of these books independently, and you will read many together. Don't be too eager to lose the one-on-one reading time either. Many sources recommend that parents continue reading to their children well past the time they become accomplished readers, and we agree!

Reading Together

Most of us probably have a deep sense that reading to kids is a good choice. But do you know why?

There are dozens of appealing reasons, but let me just remind you of the 3 highlighted by the American Academy of Pediatrics (AAP):

1. Strengthen language skills
2. Build literacy development and interest in reading
3. Create nurturing parent-child relationships, which are "important for a child's cognitive, language, and social-emotional development"

1. Language Skills

Reading exposes your child to familiar and unfamiliar words, scenes, and feelings as you give words to each of them. As he gets older and the books become more complex, he'll also be learning syntax, pronunciation, rhyming, and more!

2. Literacy Development

Your child is seeing that books are engaging and important to you. You are also demonstrating that they are interesting and a worthy use of time. This is such critical knowledge!

3. Nurturing Parent-Child Relationships

Surely we aren't the only ones who have stared at our darling child feeling like we have already done all the things and wondering how in the world we will fill the remaining time in the day. What if instead of screen time or pleading with him to play by himself, you reached happily for a book? Can you imagine how much bonding and conversation could fill in the gaps of your day?

Now, we know all too well that there are moments when children do need to play independently, for both your sanity and theirs. And if you're blessed with more than one little one (as our family is), you can't sit and read as much of the day as you'd prefer. But every minute of reading you squeeze in cultivates your relationship with your precious child without much in-the-moment effort on your part!

4. Emotional Intelligence

We've added this point to the AAP's list. Emotional intelligence is a critical skill yet challenging to teach. Reading together is an easy way to teach emotional intelligence in an unlimited variety of contexts. This not only helps your child become more fluent in his own feelings but also develops empathy and understanding for the people around him.

How It Works

On each week's challenge page (beginning on page 152), you'll find 3 things:
- A list of suggested book titles
- A place to write in the titles you read together
- A chart to track your progress through the reading challenge.

You will set your own pace this year, ranging from 1 to 5 books per week. Choose a reading goal early in the year and set your pace accordingly, keeping in mind what is realistic for your family this year.

Here's the pace for a 36-week schedule:

- Light Reader: 1 book every week (36 total)
- Interested Reader: 2 books every week (72 total)
- Avid Reader: 3 books every week (108 total)
- Committed Reader: 4 books every week (144 total)
- Enthralled Reader: 5 books every week (180 total)

But I Don't Have Any Idea Which Books to Choose!

We have your back! Beginning on page 152 you'll find thousands of book ideas you'll love this year.

If you want more ideas, we highly recommend your local librarian, the Read-Aloud Revival podcast, and the Timberdoodle Facebook groups as excellent starting points. It's also a wonderful idea to peek at the additional reading ideas in your history or science textbooks—particularly if your child found he was fascinated by something his courses recently touched on.

What about Reading Level?

This year we're providing you with a range of titles. Many are are designed for early readers while others range from chapter books designed to be read to your child to picture books to enjoy together. Pick and choose the titles and styles you think will work best for your child, but we'd also suggest adding a few books to your library list from outside your normal selection. (E.g., if your child gravitates to books he can read himself, make sure you also include some more complex books for you to read aloud.) Why? Children rarely enjoy only one type of book. They just may not know what they like yet! In light of that, we highly encourage you to intentionally expose your child to a broad spectrum of literature and see what stands out to you both.

Will This Be Expensive?

It doesn't need to be. You can read library books and e-books, buy used, borrow from friends, and scour your family bookshelves. Don't forget that many libraries have free e-books as well. If you have Kindle Unlimited or Everand, check for these titles there also. It doesn't get much more convenient than that!

Before You Begin

Please note that you do not need to complete these challenges in order! We highly recommend using the seasonal ones as close to the appropriate holiday as your schedule allows. Or if your child is all about reptiles this week, there is no need to wait until week 21 to study them.

It is also OK to skip or substitute topics. Perhaps your child is well-versed in farms but would love to learn about specific artists. Or on a deeper level, some of our young children in foster care would enjoy books about family, while others would find them triggering. It's totally appropriate to substitute a book about wild animal parents or whatever makes it more appropriate and interesting for your child.

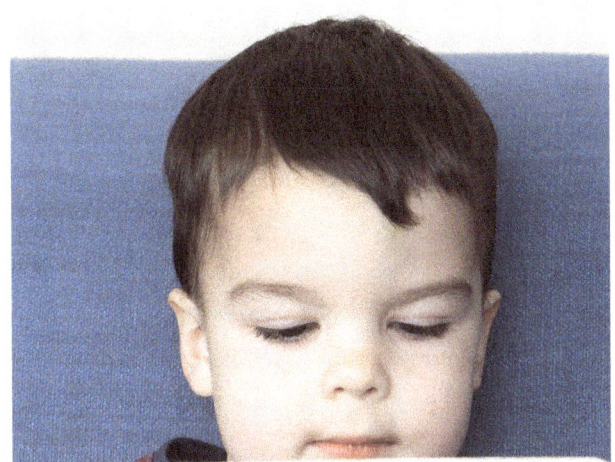

Photo: The Arnal Family in Colorado

Extra Activities

On the following pages you'll find additional ideas our team has brainstormed that may be helpful for your family. If you're looking for field trip ideas, art inspiration, or a theme for the week, use these. If your week is quite busy enough, skip them! They are not essential—just bonus ideas if you have extra time this week or want to meet a field trip goal.

Let's Read!

Pick your plan, choose some books with your child, and get started!

Looking for more reading challenges? Check out RedeemedReader.com and Challies.com for their original versions of this reading challenge. It has been completely remodeled by us over the years but was initially inspired by them and used with permission.

Tiny Tots Overview

These are Just Foundations. Tweak to Your Child's Needs!

If you took every tool out of your kit and put it to use each week, this is what your annual planner and weekly checklist could look like.

Most tiny ones develop in such a way that they outgrow some tools before growing into others. For instance, the Stacking Rocket won't likely be used at the same time that you're working on your newborn's tummy time!

So go ahead and finish reading the pages for your child's developmental age before you work out your own schedule.

We've consolidated books (including the emotional intelligence book) under a single "reading" entry because that is what would make the most sense in our family schedule. If that's not ideal for you, then by all means change it!

You'll find one other areas where we've combined tools on your list: under sensory skills. Again, if this approach works as well for your family as it does for ours—yay! If not, customize your own schedule online.

Photo: Maxwell

Included in Reading:

Indestructibles Social Studies Set

Visual Perception Collection

L is for Lion

Baby Babble Collection

100 First Words: Nature

Baby Gym books

My First Peter and the Wolf

A to Z: An Alphabet of Animals

Ditty Bird Collection

First Words Around the Home

Making Faces: A First Book of Emotions

Pat-A-Cake

Your Annual Planner

Curriculum	Lesson or Pages	= Per Week
Guide		
Active Baby, Healthy Brain	135 exercises	daily
Language Arts		
Baby Sign Language Flash Cards	50 signs	2 new cards
Touch and Feel Cards: Animals / First Words	32 flashcards	daily
Reading	19 books included	daily
Flower Whistle	unlimited	twice a week
Math		
Junior Rainbow Pebbles	unlimited	twice a week
STEM		
Sensory Spinners	unlimited	as desired
Happy World Fruit Delivery	unlimited	twice a week
Match the Buddies	12 puzzles	twice a week
Faces Puzzles	1 puzzle	once a week
Baby Popi	unlimited	once a week
SmartMax Baby STEM	unlimited	twice a week
PlanToys Stacking Rocket	unlimited	once a week

Emotional Intelligence

Making Faces book (scheduled with reading)	unlimited	weekly
Peeka Mirror	unlimited	daily
Bébé Doll	unlimited	twice a week
Playmobil Community	unlimited	twice a week
Nins Neighborhood	unlimited	twice a week

Motor Skills

Baby Gym books (scheduled with reading)	unlimited	weekly
Gymnic Physio Roll	unlimited	3 times a week
Pat-A-Cake (scheduled with reading)	1 book	once a week
Gymnic Over Ball	unlimited	3 times a week

Sensory Skills

Sensory Play	unlimited	daily
Hexagonal Teether	unlimited	as desired
Lil' Dimpl	unlimited	as desired
Peek & Pull Baby Tissue Box	unlimited	scheduled as sensory play
Playsilk	unlimited	scheduled as sensory play
Zippee	unlimited	scheduled as sensory play

Sample Weekly Checklist

<mark>Infant</mark>

Curriculum	This Week	Check It Off!
Guide		
Active Baby, Healthy Brain	daily	☐ ☐ ☐ ☐ ☐
Language Arts		
Baby Sign Language Flash Cards	2 new cards	☐ ☐
Touch and Feel Cards: Animals / First Words	daily	☐ ☐ ☐ ☐ ☐
Reading	daily	☐ ☐ ☐ ☐ ☐
STEM		
Sensory Spinners	as desired	☐
Happy World Fruit Delivery	twice a week	☐ ☐
Emotional Intelligence		
Making Faces book (scheduled with reading)	weekly	☐
Peeka Mirror	daily	☐ ☐ ☐ ☐ ☐
Motor Skills		
Baby Gym books (scheduled with reading)	weekly	☐
Gymnic Physio Roll	3 times a week	☐ ☐ ☐
Sensory Skills		
Hexagonal Teether	as desired	☐
Lil' Dimpl	as desired	☐
Peek & Pull Baby Tissue Box	twice a week	☐ ☐
Playsilk	twice a week	☐ ☐
Zippee	as desired	☐

Sample Weekly Checklist

Toddler

Curriculum	This Week	Check It Off!
Guide		
Active Baby, Healthy Brain	daily	☐ ☐ ☐ ☐ ☐
Language Arts		
Reading	daily	☐ ☐ ☐ ☐ ☐
Flower Whistle	twice a week	☐ ☐
Math		
Junior Rainbow Pebbles	twice a week	☐ ☐
STEM		
Match the Buddies	twice a week	☐ ☐
Faces Puzzles	once a week	☐
Baby Popi	once a week	☐
SmartMax Baby STEM	twice a week	☐ ☐
PlanToys Stacking Rocket	once a week	☐
Emotional Intelligence		
Bébé Doll	twice a week	☐ ☐
Playmobil Community	twice a week	☐ ☐
Nins Neighborhood	twice a week	☐ ☐
Motor Skills		
Pat-A-Cake (scheduled with reading)	once a week	☐
Gymnic Over Ball	3 times a week	☐ ☐ ☐

Sample Weekly Checklist

Birth to 2

Curriculum	This Week	Check It Off!
Guide		
Active Baby, Healthy Brain	daily	☐ ☐ ☐ ☐ ☐
Language Arts		
Baby Sign Language Flash Cards	2 new cards	☐ ☐
Touch and Feel Cards: Animals / First Words	daily	☐ ☐ ☐ ☐ ☐
Reading	daily	☐ ☐ ☐ ☐ ☐
Flower Whistle	twice a week	☐ ☐
Math		
Junior Rainbow Pebbles	twice a week	☐ ☐
STEM		
Sensory Spinners	as desired	☐
Happy World Fruit Delivery	twice a week	☐ ☐
Match the Buddies	twice a week	☐ ☐
Faces Puzzles	once a week	☐
Baby Popi	once a week	☐
SmartMax Baby STEM	twice a week	☐ ☐
PlanToys Stacking Rocket	once a week	☐

Emotional Intelligence

Making Faces book (scheduled with reading)	weekly	
Peeka Mirror	daily	
Bébé Doll	twice a week	
Playmobil Community	twice a week	
Nins Neighborhood	twice a week	

Motor Skills

Baby Gym books (scheduled with reading)	weekly
Gymnic Physio Roll	3 times a week
Pat-A-Cake (scheduled with reading)	once a week
Gymnic Over Ball	3 times a week

Sensory Skills

Hexagonal Teether	as desired
Lil' Dimpl	as desired
Peek & Pull Baby Tissue Box	twice a week
Playsilk	twice a week
Zippee	as desired

Weekly Checklists Age-by-Age

Planning By Developmental Age

Before we get into the details on each item, it will be helpful to break it down by age range. Our expectations for a toddler are much different than those for a newborn!

Keep in mind here that you will care more about developmental age than you do about chronological age. Your advanced 10-month-old may be ready for some of the work typically reserved for 13 months and up, or your premature now-6-month-old may still be developmentally 3 months old. Flex with your child, and don't be in a rush to advance him unless he is bored with the current activities.

Also, if your child is completing a more advanced level keep an eye on the *Active Baby, Healthy Brain* warnings. You'll want to make sure that you don't pick activities that his body isn't ready for, even if his brain is eager to go to the next level!

Newborn Through 3 Months

Cuddling and Nurturing for Brain Development

Every Touch Grows His Brain

Recent studies are proving again and again that the single most impactful thing you can do for your newborn's development is to pick him up. Holding him helps him regulate his system and, fascinatingly, strengthens his neural network. What does this mean for you? Well, if he has a fussy day and you are barely able to set him down long enough to use the bathroom—let alone enough to get through his list—don't worry! You're already doing the most important thing. If you baby-wear, he will also receive much-needed vestibular input as you move throughout your day. And don't get us started on the auditory, visual, and connection advantages!

Set These Things Aside

We expect that the flashcards, teethers, and Sensory Spinners are a bit much for this age. You may want to set these aside for just a few months.

Reading

Yes, it seems a little ridiculous to read with someone who can't even focus his eyes, but this really is helpful! Reading increases your child's auditory processing skills, visual perception, language development, connection, and so much more. Read a book from your kit, the library, or your bookshelf. Content matters little at this stage; what you're looking for is the experience.

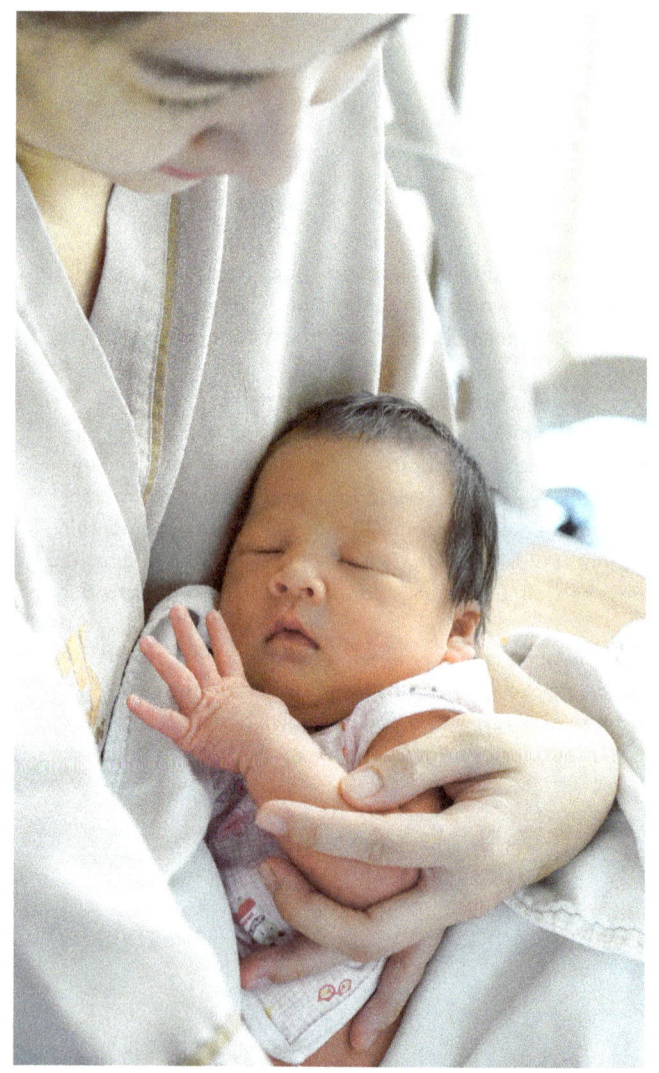

Sensory Input

The Playsilk can be used as often as every day, by gently rubbing/brushing/rolling on your baby's skin. The frequent exposure helps your little one learn to process sensations all over his body, while also helping with bonding and so much more. Add as many other gentle textures as you can and watch his brain grow! Many delightful textures can be found in the Peek & Pull Baby Tissue Box.

Auditory Processing

Any baby toy with a sound in it may be used for auditory processing. Rattle, squeak, or crinkle them where your child has to turn his head slightly to see them. As his skills improve, you'll be able to place them farther away and squeak/rattle them less before he focuses on them. You'll find that the crinkly Baby Papers that accompany the Peek & Pull Baby Tissue Box are a great resource.

Tummy Time

We've had many little ones with acid reflux, which is miserable for all parties. But did you know that tummy time strengthens the core muscles that actually work to structurally solve reflux? If your little one can't tolerate direct tummy time yet, look into baby wearing or other ways to strengthen those muscles and get you both some relief! As your baby gets some head strength, set up Happy World Fruit Delivery and prop open his books for him to enjoy as he looks around.

Case #1: Elias

Sweet baby Elias is 2 weeks old and was discharged from the NICU today. You notice that he is very jumpy to any sounds and cries at even gentle touches.

In addition to cuddling and wearing him as much as possible, you'll want to emphasize as much sensory input as you can. Touch him softly (with warm hands) as often as possible. Consider parking soft, textured items and your favorite lotion at the changing table. After each change (or every other) strip him down to his diaper and stroke/lotion him while singing/talking to him. Use the auditory tools in your toolbox (rattles, squeakers, etc.) to help him become less and less startled by common sounds.

At two weeks, Elias isn't ready to hold anything and certainly isn't teething, so we'll remove the teethers from his list. We'll also adjust the number of times per week so that he is doing auditory exercises every day, adding in any rattles or interesting noises from around the house.

Case #2: Halona

At three months, you notice that Halona really lacks muscle strength. She cries during tummy time and is flacid as you pick her up.

For Halona you're going to want to emphasize gross motor skills as much as you can. Revisit your *Active Baby, Healthy Brain* checklist and buckle down to complete as much of the chart as possible each week.

Try putting her Peeka Mirror at the changing table (Hey, we know you'll be hanging out there a lot!) and see if she can be on her stomach for exactly one minute after each diaper change. When that is achievable without stressing her out, increase it to two minutes, etc. Soon you'll be able to move her to the floor without making her cry!

Knowing you really need to work on gross motor skills this month, put that at the top of your priority list. However, if you have enough time in the day, you'll try to accomplish all her goals. She's ready!

Case #3: Ranger

Tiny Ranger is one month old, still in newborn sizes, and experienced prenatal drug exposure. He cries a lot and seems very stiff with frantic, jerky motions.

Ranger needs help regulating his body. (Swaddling, while not a point of our kit, is worth noting, as it can be hugely helpful!) For him, you will likely be modifying many of the sensory activities. You want it to almost be too much for him but never to cross that line.

Newborns and tiny ones usually start sneezing/coughing/yawning when they are beginning to be stressed, so keep an eye on that as a possible early-warning sign of becoming overwhelmed. (Of course, they do all these things for normal physiological reasons too!)

If you find that putting on lotion makes him frantic, try warming your hands under hot water first, slowing your motions, etc. You want his abilities to be growing without adding more stress to his life, especially since much of his day is taken up with just getting calories in him right now.

For some babies, the cuddling/rocking/swaying/singing that we instinctively do to help them calm down is in itself distressing. (This is particularly true of drug-exposed infants or babies with a lot of NICU time.) If he becomes extremely overwrought, try swaddling him, giving him a pacifier, and setting him in his crib in a quiet, dark room, minimizing the sensory input he's receiving. As he calms down, pick him up and keep him at arm's length, drawing him to yourself as he allows.

In calm times, work on rocking him gently until he begins to show the earliest signs of stress, then stop. Slowly but surely, you're rewiring his brain! (Some babies prefer to be rocked while they are held vertically, while others prefer more traditional rocking. Work with your baby to find his unique preferences!)

Ranger's schedule looks a lot like Elias's on paper. Both little boys need a focus on sensory integration, even though the depth of their need is quite different.

You'll also be tweaking these activities more for Ranger than you would need to for Elias. For instance, Elias may be able to handle the crinkly sounds of Baby Paper at close range, while Ranger is only ready for the tiniest sound at several feet away. Both versions deserve a check-off, though—you've done what was appropriate for YOUR little one!

0-3 Months Resources

Weekly Checklist

Curriculum	This Week	Check It Off!
Guide		
Active Baby, Healthy Brain	daily	☐ ☐ ☐ ☐ ☐
Language Arts		
Reading	daily	☐ ☐ ☐ ☐ ☐
STEM		
Happy World Fruit Delivery	twice a week	☐ ☐
Emotional Intelligence		
Making Faces book (scheduled with reading)	weekly	☐
Peeka Mirror	daily	☐ ☐ ☐ ☐ ☐
Motor Skills		
Gymnic Physio Roll	3 times a week	☐ ☐ ☐
Sensory Skills		
Hexagonal Teether	as desired	☐
Lil' Dimpl	as desired	☐
Peek & Pull Baby Tissue Box	twice a week	☐ ☐
Playsilk	twice a week	☐ ☐

0-3 Months Active Baby, Healthy Brain
Weekly Checklist

Basic Exercises

	Mon.	Tues.	Wed.	Thurs.	Fri.
Slowly massage front & back					
Tummy time (5 days+)					
Leg flexing (2-3 months+)					
Rocking sideways					
Gentle turnovers					
Arm movements					
Back pushaways					
Tummy time over a roll					
Tummy pushaways (4 weeks+)					
Rolling (2 months+)					
Feet & leg reflexes (2 months+)					
Neck & back strengthening (2 months+)					
Rocking forward (parachute reflex)					
Hitting / kicking a hanging balloon (2 months+)					

Vestibular Stimulation

	Mon.	Tues.	Wed.	Thurs.	Fri.
Slightly inflated big ball					
Seated rocking from side to side					
Hammock swing					
Stroller ride on bumpy ground					
Stand and rock (2 months+)					
Bobbing up & down (2 months+)					
Rocking, rolling, bouncing on your knees (2 months+)					
Rocking back and forth (2-3 months+)					
Rolling on a ball (3 months+)					
Extreme rocking on your knees (3 months+) 10 times					
"Here We Go Side to Side" (3 months+)					

Music, Rhythm, and Song

	Mon.	Tues.	Wed.	Thurs.	Fri.
Music & nature sounds					
Stories, rhymes, and "conversations"					
Dancing (head supported)					
Bouncing and swaying on his front (4 weeks+)					
Action rhymes (6 weeks+)					

Vision

	Mon.	Tues.	Wed.	Thurs.	Fri.
Flickering lights (0-2 months) 4 times/day					
Tracking rattle sounds					

4-6 Months

Becoming Aware of Everything

Break Out Some New Tools

You will want to bring out the Lil' Dimpl and Hexagonal Teether now if you haven't already. You may or may not want to pull out the Sensory Spinners as well. While it will be some time before your baby gets the full advantage of the suction cups, he is getting old enough to enjoy the rattling, chewing, and novel shape.

Flashcards?

As soon as your baby begins to sit up (usually by 7 months), he's definitely ready to enjoy the flashcards, but we mention them here since some 4- to 6-month-olds are also eager to move to this type of interaction. We'd suggest breaking them out once a month or so until you find your baby is ready.

Reading

Definitely keep up with the daily reading time. As mentioned before, reading increases auditory processing skills, visual perception, language development, connection, and so much more. Read a book from your kit, the library, or your bookshelf. Content matters little at this stage; what you're looking for is the experience.

Tummy Time or Floor Time?

When baby starts crawling, tummy time transitions to floor time whether you're ready or not! It is still important to encourage as much time spent horizontal as possible. As baby moves his body, he's gaining tons of sensory input and learning where his body is in space. He's also strengthening his back and upper body, which oddly enough will help even with digestion. (It turns out that as those muscles develop, his internal core also develops, including the muscles that minimize reflux.)

Sensory Input

Soft sensory items such as the Playsilk should still come out to play often, as you gently rub, brush, or roll it on your baby's skin. The frequent exposure helps your little one learn to process sensations all over his body, while also helping with bonding and so much more. Add as many other gentle textures as you can and watch his brain grow!

Auditory Processing

Baby Paper, the Sensory Spinners, or other toys you already own that have a sound to them may be used for auditory processing. Rattle or squeak them where your child has to turn his head to see them. At this age he'll be able to track better and farther than he could just a few short months ago.

Case #1: Violet

Four-month-old Violet is so easygoing and happy that she's the kind of baby that makes other parents jealous. However, you wonder if she's "too easy" since she seems quite content to just lie back and watch the action.

Violet is every parent's dream baby, so on one hand, we encourage you to relax and soak up all these moments.

On the other hand, we want to encourage you to make sure that her easygoing temperament isn't masking low muscle tone or disinterest in the world around her. You'll want to emphasize gross motor skills and monitor her development to make sure all seems well. But you're also going to want to treasure the sweet delight that she is! No modifications needed for her list.

Case #2: Santiago

Busy Santiago was born with a club foot and must wear his brace 23 hours a day. He doesn't seem to mind, but at 6 months old, he is a bit behind his peers in gross motor skills. The brace makes Santiago a little more challenging for you to carry and set in certain seats. With a little accommodation and attention, however, you'll find that he is still able to be a part of most adventures.

You are going to want to keep a particular eye on his vestibular development, as the temptation will be to set him down more than a "free and clear" baby. His access to sensory activities will also be more limited with the brace in place. Ideally, you'll be able to use his hour off each day not only to bathe him but also to get him some of that sensory input, especially to his feet. Perhaps you could grab the squares from the Peek & Pull Baby Tissue Box, or the Playsilk, and do some fun foot massages right after his bath?

You're not going to need to change Santiago's plan on paper, but you're definitely going to need to modify the exercises to make them all work for him. Some of that will be by moving activities to his brace-free time, while for others you'll just put his legs in the best possible position and live with the "not quite as pictured in the book" accommodation.

The most useful thing you could probably do would be to schedule his hour with free feet to be an hour you would be most likely to get one-on-one time with him—perhaps naptime or quiet reading time for everyone else?

Case #3: Jade

Sadly, five-month-old baby Jade has suffered some severe brain damage in her life. Whether this was because of a stroke, shaken baby syndrome, or some other trauma, this is definitely going to impact her development.

The wonderful thing is that infants are wired to have rapidly developing brains even if they have been damaged. You will want to capitalize on this by investing as much time and energy as possible into Jade. Adjust the exercises as much as she needs to make them doable for her.

Often infants with trauma need extra sleep to help their brains heal. If this is the case for Jade, do what you can to help her get all the rest she needs. It will be as important to her as her waking hours are!

With Jade's delays, she is operating at roughly a 2-month-old level physically and developmentally. In light of that, just flip back to the weekly planner for 0-3 months.

This month you'll want to work hard at the activities she's ready for, while encouraging as much sleep and connection as you can.

4-6 Months Resources

Weekly Checklist

Curriculum	This Week	Check It Off!
Guide		
Active Baby, Healthy Brain	daily	☐☐☐☐☐
Language Arts		
Baby Sign Language Flash Cards	2 new cards	☐☐☐☐
Touch and Feel Cards: Animals / First Words	daily	☐☐☐☐☐☐
Reading	daily	☐☐☐☐☐☐
STEM		
Sensory Spinners	as desired	☐
Happy World Fruit Delivery	twice a week	☐☐
Emotional Intelligence		
Making Faces book (scheduled with reading)	weekly	☐
Peeka Mirror	daily	☐☐☐☐☐
Motor Skills		
Baby Gym books (scheduled with reading)	weekly	☐
Gymnic Physio Roll	3 times a week	☐☐☐
Sensory Skills		
Hexagonal Teether	as desired	☐
Lil' Dimpl	as desired	☐
Peek & Pull Baby Tissue Box	twice a week	☐☐
Playsilk	twice a week	☐☐
Zippee	as desired	☐

4-6 Months Active Baby, Healthy Brain

Weekly Checklist

Basic Exercises

	Mon.	Tues.	Wed.	Thurs.	Fri.
Slowly massage front & back					
Tummy time					
Leg flexing					
Rocking sideways					
Gentle turnovers					
Arm movements					
Back pushaways					
Tummy time over a roll					
Tummy pushaways					
Rolling					
Feet & leg reflexes					
Neck & back strengthening					
Rocking forward (parachute reflex)					
Hitting / kicking a hanging balloon					

Upper Body

Pull-ups					
Push-ups					

Vestibular Stimulation

	Mon.	Tues.	Wed.	Thurs.	Fri.
Slightly inflated big ball					
Seated rocking from side to side					
Hammock swing					
Stroller ride on bumpy ground					
Stand and rock					
Bobbing up & down					
Rocking, rolling, bouncing on your knees					
Rocking back and forth					
Rolling on a ball					
Extreme rocking on your knees 10 times					
"Here We Go Side to Side"					

Music, Rhythm, and Song

	Mon.	Tues.	Wed.	Thurs.	Fri.
Music & nature sounds					
Stories, rhymes, and "conversations"					
Dancing (head supported)					
Bouncing and swaying on his front					
Action rhymes					

7-9 Months

Getting Baby on the Move

Let's Start Signing!

Technically we don't emphasize signing until 12 months, but we've found that many babies are ready to begin a slow introduction to the concept somewhere around 7 months old.

Are you ready to build your child's communication skills? This is going to be so fun! You'll begin by modeling the signs and then immediately help your child copy you. For instance, sign "milk" before feeding him, then take his hand in yours and help him sign it in some fashion. Immediately give him the milk he was "asking" for. Some babies will pick up on this easily, while for others it will take some time.

Expect him to start getting it after a month or two, but don't be shocked if it's shorter or longer.

Here are our favorite words to begin with: milk or water, more, book, sleep, please, and all done. We use the milk or water sign for liquids of all kinds—water may be easier for some babies to sign.

Set These Things Aside

If you have the Infant Kit only, nothing! You'll be using everything in your Infant Kit at this point.

If You Have the Birth to 2 Kit

Your child will likely already get a lot of enjoyment out of a few of the toddler items, such as the books and the Gymnic Over Ball. You may also find that he's ready for the Bébé doll or the Flower Whistle, but that would be a little more rare.

Reading

Your baby will benefit so much from daily reading time in these months. As mentioned before, reading increases auditory processing skills, visual perception, language development, connection, and so much more. Read a book from your kit, the library, or your bookshelf...just make sure you're reading together.

Don't Forget Sensory Input

This can still be as simple as using the Playsilk or other soft items daily by gently rubbing/brushing on his skin to help him learn to process sensations all over his body. Add as many other gentle textures as you can and watch his brain grow. Grass, sand, gravel, carpets, blankets...that's all sensory play. Bath time is also a sensory experience for him, as is mealtime!

Case #1: Sebastian

At 8 months old, little Sebastian clearly seems to be in the genius category—if there is such a thing. He can sign half a dozen words readily, learns new ones rapidly, and uses them appropriately. He babbles and nearly forms words. He's also progressed rapidly from crawling to already beginning to walk. You feel like this is the shortest babyhood ever!

First off, congratulations! You're obviously pouring into Sebastian's life, and his abilities showcase that. So the first thing to do is just keep doing what you're doing!

Second, try to take a step back and see what areas he is weak in compared to the rest of his development. For instance, if all the other newly walking tiny ones in his play group are better at recognizing emotions than he is ("Can you make a sad face, Sebastian?"), then prioritize that over increasing his strengths only.

At the same time, you do want to capitalize on his strengths. If he's wired like a gymnast, find a safe way for him to climb to his heart's content. Or if he's a born book-lover, invest in trips to the library and hours spent soaking up books together. You want to encourage his giftedness in all areas.

For his checklist, there is no need to stay at an 8-month level. Instead, jump right ahead to 9-12 months since those activities are most appropriate to his skills and abilities. Don't forget to ease into any activities that he finds tricky. You want to challenge and engage him but definitely not overwhelm him!

One Note:
Don't be discouraged or deflated if Sebastian becomes more "average" over time. One beauty of homeschooling is the ability to customize what he's learning to what he's ready for right now. When his growth curve settles down to a normal pace, adjust your expectations accordingly and continue to enjoy your time together.

Case #2: Elle

Elle arrived to your home as a darling 7-month-old with an unfortunate history of severe neglect. She is very content to stay in one spot and has a giant flat spot on the back of her head. She seems developmentally to be about 4 months old, despite her chronological age.

As you probably suspected, you will want to adjust Elle's plan to her developmental age—4 months. You will likely find that in a few weeks she is making unprecedented progress across all fields, so reevaluate often, but start with the 4-month checklists so you don't miss any important developmental steps.

You will particularly want to make sure that Elle is spending as little time on her back as possible. Her doctor will advise if she needs a helmet or other interventions, but if you limit her back time to sleeping only, that will also begin to help. While it is a bit off the topic of homeschooling, we'd also encourage as much baby-wearing as Elle can tolerate. It will help with her flat spot and, more importantly, reintegrate her into family life.

Case #3: Wilder

As you carried sweet 9-month-old Wilder into your house 2 weeks ago, you experienced every parent's nightmare as you slipped and fell on your steps. Wilder ended up with a femur fracture that is already healing well, but his physical abilities this month are limited.

Wilder is going to end up with a few deficits from this experience, and that is OK. There is a lot you can do to keep him on target and even give him an edge in some areas. The other developmental milestones will come later after his cast is off and normal life resumes.

You'll want to keep his list the same but be heavily editing many of the physical activities to suit the particulars of his cast and pain level.

7-9 Months Resources

Weekly Checklist

Curriculum	This Week	Check It Off!
Guide		
Active Baby, Healthy Brain	daily	
Language Arts		
Baby Sign Language Flash Cards	2 new cards	
Touch and Feel Cards: Animals / First Words	daily	
Reading	daily	
STEM		
Sensory Spinners	as desired	
Happy World Fruit Delivery	twice a week	
Emotional Intelligence		
Making Faces book (scheduled with reading)	weekly	
Peeka Mirror	daily	
Motor Skills		
Baby Gym books (scheduled with reading)	weekly	
Gymnic Physio Roll	3 times a week	
Sensory Skills		
Hexagonal Teether	as desired	
Lil' Dimpl	as desired	
Peek & Pull Baby Tissue Box	twice a week	
Playsilk	twice a week	
Zippee	as desired	

7-9 Months Active Baby, Healthy Brain

Weekly Checklist

Massage

	Mon.	Tues.	Wed.	Thurs.	Fri.
Massage					
Massage with textures					
Warm vs. cold water					

Basic Exercises

Tummy time (toys, books, mirror, noises)					
Crocodile crawling					
Stairs					
Obstacle courses (including under furniture)					
Getting out of a box					
Bobbing down for toys					
Hold on, stand, and kick with one foot					

Upper Body

Row, Row, Row Your Boat (head lowered, hands grip)					
Wheelbarrow					
Rolling over a small ball					

Vestibular Stimulation

	Mon.	Tues.	Wed.	Thurs.	Fri.
Rocking on a big ball (front, back, all ways)					
Sitting on a roll (or peanut ball / Physio Roll)					
Flying on your legs					
Toddler swing					
Riding or rocking on your legs					

Music, Rhythm, and Song

	Mon.	Tues.	Wed.	Thurs.	Fri.
Hide-and-seek-music					

Vision

	Mon.	Tues.	Wed.	Thurs.	Fri.
Visual tracking					
Posting (items go out of sight)					
Word cards & matching					

Sensory Activities

	Mon.	Tues.	Wed.	Thurs.	Fri.
Rolling in a blanket					
Swinging in a blanket					
Rolling down slopes					
Crawling on / exploring new surfaces (prickly / soft grass, paths, sand, dirt…)					
Pots & pans					
Creeping up and rolling down slopes					
Creeping over a raised surface					
Climbing up or creeping along a ladder					

10-12 Months
Eager to Talk and Walk

Communication Is Key

One wonderful thing about teaching your child sign language is that once he learns the principles of communication, he will often shock you by beginning to talk instead. Know that the sign language you do now will likely pay off big time in months to come.

You'll also likely find that the more words he has (spoken or signed), the more content and happy he is. After all, if he is able to express his desires, that will eliminate much of the frustration and stress in his daily life.

To help him begin to master words, encourage him to make sounds while signing. Any attempt at imitation should be celebrated, and as he progresses you'll ask for more and more precision (that's a long way off, though).

If this is his first time being exposed to signs, you will want to start by modeling the signs to him and then help him copy them. For instance, sign "banana" before giving him a bite of one, then help him sign it with his hands—no precision required! Immediately give him the banana he was "asking" for to solidify the concept. As mentioned previously, some babies will pick up on this easily, while for others it will take some time. Expect him to start getting it after a month or two, but don't be shocked if it's shorter or longer.

Set These Things Aside

If you have the Infant Kit, nothing! You'll be using everything in your Infant Kit at this time.

If You Have the Tiny Tots Birth to 2 Kit (0-24 months)

Even though these items were selected for 12 months and up, your child may be ready now to get a lot of enjoyment out of them:
All books
Gymnic Over Ball
Flower Whistle
Bébé Doll
SmartMax Baby STEM

Reading

Your baby will continue to benefit so much from daily reading time. As mentioned before, reading increases auditory processing skills, visual perception, language development, connection, and so much more. Read a book from your kit, the library, or your bookshelf...just make sure you're reading together.

Don't Forget Sensory Input

This can still be as simple as using soft items such as the Playsilk daily by gently rubbing/brushing/rolling on his skin to help him learn to process sensations all over his body. Add as many other gentle textures as you can and watch his brain grow. Grass, sand, gravel, carpets, blankets...that's all sensory play. Bath time is also a sensory experience for him, as is mealtime!

Case #1: Meadow, Skye, River

Yep, there are three names there. Congratulations on your 10-month-old triplets! Your amazing little ones were delivered early and spent some time in the NICU, so 10 months is their adjusted age. Now that they are getting mobile, you will have even less one-on-one time with your babies, so what can you do to set them up for happy and healthy development?

First, relax. Yes, their life will look different from Arrow's (below), as would the life of a child added to a large family. They will learn from and enjoy their siblings so much in these months, and they will teach each other in their "down time," Talk about peer pressure!

A high priority for you is going to be implementation. What can you do to make these months' checklists easy to implement? Consider where you put the checklists (Fridge? Play area? Changing table?) and your routine for completing items. It may be more achievable to do Gymnic Physio Roll with all three, one after another, rather than working River through his entire list for the day while his sisters play. You also may find a single list more efficient than managing three separate papers.

Because they have NICU history, it is likely that they have some sensory processing challenges. In that case, add "sensory" to your daily list, knowing that this could be as simple as playing on the grass in a onesie or as involved as cooking "just for play" spaghetti and letting them have a blast squashing, squeezing, and tasting it. Crawl-through tunnels are also great for sensory processing because of the visual and vestibular input they provide.

Case #2: Arrow

Ten-month-old Arrow is your first child, and you have the freedom to be a stay-at-home parent with no other commitments. Why not invest as much time as possible into his development?

For him, you'll be using a standard list, but add in trips to the zoo, aquarium, parks, and the children's museum. You will also want to work toward letting him enjoy playing independently. Do all that you can to foster connection and enjoyment of each other, but you'll also want him to have the skill of independent exploring. Working up to at least 15 minutes of solo play is appropriate for this age group. Of course, you aren't abandoning your child or isolating him—just realizing that this is yet another skill for him to learn that isn't on the list.

Case #3: Emily

As Emily approaches her first birthday, you notice that she doesn't use her right arm as well or as easily as she does her left. Signing is difficult, and even when she's beginning to walk you notice that her balance seems off. She's finally diagnosed with Brachial Plexus, and all the symptoms begin to make sense.

While Emily's checklist won't change, you will want to add in any exercises that her physical therapist and occupational therapist recommend. Of course, you'll prioritize those over her routine activities to aid in her healing. The great news is that she is very likely to fully recover from this injury!

10-12 Months Resources

Weekly Checklist

Curriculum	This Week	Check It Off!
Guide		
Active Baby, Healthy Brain	daily	
Language Arts		
Baby Sign Language Flash Cards	2 new cards	
Touch and Feel Cards: Animals / First Words	daily	
Reading	daily	
STEM		
Sensory Spinners	as desired	
Happy World Fruit Delivery	twice a week	
Emotional Intelligence		
Making Faces book (scheduled with reading)	weekly	
Peeka Mirror	daily	
Motor Skills		
Baby Gym books (scheduled with reading)	weekly	
Gymnic Physio Roll	3 times a week	
Sensory Skills		
Hexagonal Teether	as desired	
Lil' Dimpl	as desired	
Peek & Pull Baby Tissue Box	twice a week	
Playsilk	twice a week	
Zippee	as desired	

10-12 Months Active Baby, Healthy Brain

Weekly Checklist

Massage

	Mon.	Tues.	Wed.	Thurs.	Fri.
Massage					
Massage with textures					
Warm vs. cold water					

Basic Exercises

	Mon.	Tues.	Wed.	Thurs.	Fri.
Tummy time (toys, books, mirror, noises)					
Crocodile crawling					
Stairs					
Obstacle courses (including under furniture)					
Getting out of a box					
Bobbing down for toys					
Hold on, stand, and kick with one foot					

Upper Body

	Mon.	Tues.	Wed.	Thurs.	Fri.
Row, Row, Row Your Boat (head lowered, hands grip)					
Wheelbarrow					
Rolling over a small ball					
Pull-ups (10-12 months)					

Vestibular Stimulation

	Mon.	Tues.	Wed.	Thurs.	Fri.
Rocking on a big ball (front, back, all ways)					
Sitting on a roll (or peanut ball / Physio Roll!)					
Flying on your legs					
Toddler swing					
Riding or rocking on your legs					

Music, Rhythm, and Song

	Mon.	Tues.	Wed.	Thurs.	Fri.
Hide-and-seek-music					
Following simple commands (10-12 months)					
Hold baby and dance (new holds for 10+ months)					

Vision

	Mon.	Tues.	Wed.	Thurs.	Fri.
Visual tracking					
Posting (items go out of sight)					
Word cards & matching					

Sensory Activities

	Mon.	Tues.	Wed.	Thurs.	Fri.
Rolling in a blanket					
Swinging in a blanket					
Rolling down slopes					
Crawling on / exploring new surfaces (prickly / soft grass, paths, sand, dirt…)					
Pots & pans					
Creeping up and rolling down slopes					
Creeping over a raised surface					
Climbing up or creeping along a ladder					

13-16 Months

Walking and Communicating

Communication Is Key

The biggest emphasis at this stage will almost certainly be communication. Use sign language, verbal communication, or both, but help your child communicate! By the way, this is the single most critical thing you can do to lower frustration, decrease tantrums, and increase his connection with you.

Reading

As always, your baby will continue to benefit so much from daily reading time. As mentioned before, reading increases auditory processing skills, visual perception, language development, connection, and so much more. Read a book from your kit, the library, or your bookshelf...just make sure you're reading together.

Introductory Skills

The infant items have now been removed from your list, and all the toddler items have been added. (Feel free to add back in any infant ones you're still using—we just didn't want to assume that you have them at hand for a toddler.) Keep in mind that some of the toddler items—such as Junior Rainbow Pebbles and the STEM items—will not be used fully as intended yet. Instead, you'll be introducing them and their concepts at an exploration level. You could also save them for a few more months, but some of us prefer to get them out and just start playing!

Case #1: Emmet

At 14 months old, Emmet is hilarious and engaging. He loves to be the center of attention and learns new words daily. He is a little behind in his walking, but he now walks while holding a hand and seems poised to take off soon. He is not hesitant to make his desires for certain foods or toys known and has the best facial expressions.

You will definitely spend a lot of your education time working on gross motor skills with Emmet. He's ready and eager to walk, so do everything you can to get him there. Try integrating movement into every activity. Can he walk one step to reach the next piece? "Help" you carry the book to the favorite reading spot? Items like the Gymnic Over Ball or other favorite toys can be a fun and motivating way to work on motor skills!

Case #2: Blessing

Blessing is also 14 months old, but she's an entirely different child. She loves to walk and is quite good at it, but she does not yet have any useful language. She is content to play for hours alone and loves moving things in and out of her play kitchen.

For Blessing, you really want to work on communication and connection. Look for opportunities to play together and have happy interactions, and do everything you can to build speech (spoken or signed). We're not above food bribes at this stage. Sometimes a little extra motivation will get a child going, and then you can back off the incentives as the skill becomes inherently rewarding.

Have you ever noticed that when you work with someone, you grow closer to them? You're going to work diligently at everything on her list—not because she lacks the physical skills, but because she desperately needs to build comfortable connections. This will in turn build her desire for communication.

Case #3: Anwell

Anwell is 16 months old and very affectionate. However, you've noticed some areas of concern. For instance, if you point at a favorite toy across the room, he can't follow that point to find the toy. He seems completely confused by any pretend play and spends inordinate amounts of time lining up objects in perfect lines or crying when some minor thing is changed in his world.

As you suspected, Anwell has many early warning signs of autism. Even as you dive into his education, you will also want to work with his pediatrician for a complete assessment by an autism expert, which should unlock services for you. Hopefully you'll get access to early intervention and the services that can make a remarkable impact in helping children with autism learn.

Anwell is a child with amazing potential, but it's going to take some effort to unlock his full abilities. We've taken ABA courses and have been thrilled to see its effectiveness as a tool in the toolbox. But what struck us most about that method of teaching is that it is, to oversimplify it, parenting on steroids. We were still teaching the same skills as we would otherwise; we were just breaking them down into smaller steps and doing more reps.

Anwell's checklist should be heavy on speech and social skills while the rest of his chart remains standard. Adjust this to accommodate his therapy schedule, of course!

All children benefit from a clear schedule/routine (see the article beginning on page 122). Visual cues can also be tremendously helpful for a child who may not be able to process auditory cues in a typical fashion.

Transitions are difficult for all children, but a child with autism will struggle with them even more. Although he has no concept of time yet, it can be helpful to use transitions like this:

"Anwell, in 15 minutes we will be all done with the park."

"Anwell, 10 more minutes and then we need to leave the park and go get Daddy."

"Anwell, 5 minutes until we go get Daddy."

(Timer ringing) "Anwell, it's time to leave. Would you like one last trip on the slide as we leave?"

Even though he does not yet know what "15 minutes" means, the rhythm and repetition will help him learn, and the ringing timer makes it feel like you're helping him cope rather than making an unfair decision about his future. You likely won't see much difference using this approach right away, but you'll be surprised how quickly he catches on!

Note:

Active Baby, Healthy Brain splits activities at 18 months rather than at 16 months. That's why you see the chart go through 18 months on page 56.

13-16 Months Resources

Weekly Checklist

Curriculum	This Week	Check It Off!
Guide		
Active Baby, Healthy Brain	daily	☐ ☐ ☐ ☐ ☐
Language Arts		
Reading	daily	☐ ☐ ☐ ☐ ☐
Flower Whistle	twice a week	☐ ☐
Math		
Junior Rainbow Pebbles	twice a week	☐ ☐
STEM		
Match the Buddies	twice a week	☐ ☐
Faces Puzzles	once a week	☐
Baby Popi	once a week	☐
SmartMax Baby STEM	twice a week	☐ ☐
PlanToys Stacking Rocket	once a week	☐
Emotional Intelligence		
Bébé Doll	twice a week	☐ ☐
Playmobil Community	twice a week	☐ ☐
Nins Neighborhood	twice a week	☐ ☐
Motor Skills		
Pat-A-Cake (scheduled with reading)	once a week	☐
Gymnic Over Ball	3 times a week	☐ ☐ ☐

Walking-18 Months Active Baby, Healthy Brain

Weekly Checklist

Massage

	Mon.	Tues.	Wed.	Thurs.	Fri.
Massage					
Massage with textures					
Across the midline activities					

Motor Planning

	Mon.	Tues.	Wed.	Thurs.	Fri.
Crawling on furniture					
Walking over the rungs of a ladder					
Creeping under furniture					

Upper Body

	Mon.	Tues.	Wed.	Thurs.	Fri.
Row, Row, Row Your Boat					
Monkey swing on rings					
Throwing a ball					

Vestibular Stimulation

	Mon.	Tues.	Wed.	Thurs.	Fri.
Balance on hills and slopes (no hands)					
Walking backwards/sideways					
Topsy-turvy somersault					
Parachute reflex over a ball					
Balance on a roll					
Ride on a scooter board					
Spinning					
Beach ball stretch					
Tipping backwards					
Rocking on your thighs					
Rolling down your lap					

Music, Rhythm, and Song

	Mon.	Tues.	Wed.	Thurs.	Fri.
Rhythm activity (such as maracas or pots)					
Dancing					
Bobbing					

Vision

	Mon.	Tues.	Wed.	Thurs.	Fri.
Balloon + fly swatter					
Roll the ball back and forth					
Parachute					
Reading books together					
Word & picture cards					

17-20 Months

We Have a Toddler!

Communication Is Key

The biggest emphasis of your teaching continues to be communication. Use sign language, verbal communication, or both, but help your child communicate! This stage is so much fun as your little one begins to let you in on what he's thinking and you are able to respond. Welcome to conversations!

Reading

As always, your baby will continue to benefit so much from daily reading time. As mentioned before, reading increases auditory processing skills, visual perception, language development, connection, and much more. Read a book from your kit, the library, or your bookshelf…just make sure you're reading together.

Following Directions

Have you ever felt that teaching a toddler to obey feels like a lot of work and conflict for little reward? It is a ton of work, but let us encourage you that it is time well spent.

You'll find a more in-depth discussion beginning on page 128, but for now it will suffice to mention that it is OK to expect your toddler to do something he doesn't want to do.

In our home this may occur when our toddler says he's all done. Sometimes we acknowledge that and help him down from the table. Other times we will say, "You're all done with that puzzle? OK, put one more piece in and then you can get down." We'll then help him hand over hand if he needs it and quickly get him down. This is helping him learn to finish and to realize that we are in fact listening to him and have reasonable expectations.

Choices for Communication

We also incorporate a lot of choices at this stage. Instead of choosing which puzzle he'll do today, why not get out both the Face Puzzles and the Stacking Rocket and let him choose?

Case #1: Hana

Charming Hana is an active, busy 18-month-old who lights up your household and has amazing fine motor skills. She loves collecting small treasures in a box or jar, then pulling them out again, or fitting simple puzzles together. However, she doesn't sleep well and has a lot of distress over any variance from her bedtime routine or unusual textures such as getting dirt on her hands or sitting in grass or sand. She has no words yet, and eating is challenging because there are very few foods that she will eat. She becomes very upset when any of her food spills; in fact, wetness anywhere on her body (outside her diaper) is cause for many tears. You've even seen her use a washcloth to keep her breakfast milk from dripping on her—quite the sight for this petite toddler!

Hana will benefit greatly from a few interventions. First, she sounds like a child with sensory challenges and would likely benefit from an occupational therapy assessment / intervention plan. A good therapist will not only work on giving her the skills to handle different sensations (grass, milk, a breeze…) but will also help you learn how to help her when she is overwhelmed. If you have the strength to wear her in a baby carrier, that is definitely worth trying. The tight / close feeling may give her the ability to face new experiences without being overwhelmed.

It also sounds like she has a speech deficit that would benefit a ton from early intervention / speech therapy. Again, a good therapist will help you know how to help Hana build her vocabulary so that you'll become her primary speech therapist. More vocabulary will go a long way toward reducing her anxiety.

She may even have apraxia of speech, which can sometimes be addressed quite effectively with specific speech therapy targeting. It's well worth the time to investigate the "why" behind any language delay in order to get her the help she needs ASAP.

Don't forget that you will be using each tool on her chart to also work on language. "Can you find the green Nin?" "What does your baby doll need next—a diaper or a bottle?" (with signs, if needed). "How does he feel?" If the list begins to feel burdensome instead of helpful, drop all the motor skills options down to once a week and really keep your focus on language.

Case #2: Hudson

While he is Hana's twin, handsome Hudson is in many ways her opposite. He has a rapidly growing vocabulary and loves touching all the things; he even has a good throwing arm!

However, Hudson sleeps a ton, spends a lot of time just sitting, and seems oblivious to all textures. He cries when put in the swing, doesn't appreciate light touches, and rages easily. His motor skills are also very lacking.

Would it shock you to learn that Hudson also has sensory processing issues? Hana's system is over-responsive, while Hudson's is under-responsive. Hudson also needs help processing vestibular input. If his feet are off the ground, for instance, he can't tell where he is in space and feels like you might feel if you tumbled through an avalanche and ended up head over heels with no idea which way was up. On top of that, he would greatly benefit by targeting fine motor skills.

His chart will include an emphasis on all things fine motor. Leave the vestibular activities on his chart, but anticipate that you will work with his occupational therapist to determine which ones he is ready for and which ones you should set aside for a later date. The ones that you keep on the schedule after that conversation will be heavily tailored to make them as easy as possible until he's comfortable.

For both twins you will want to do some trial and error with what's on their list. It may become natural to do one or two activities after each meal/snack. Or perhaps you could set a timer for an hour, do one activity, then reset it for another hour and repeat. Find a strategy that works for you, or completely ignore the list if he's become excited to drop raisins down a paper towel tube. After all, why pull him off the fine motor activity he chose in order to do one that may not captivate him at that moment?

Note:

Active Baby, Healthy Brain splits lists at 18 months, rather than 17 months. We're using the 18-24 month section here, but we wouldn't hesitate to use the 12-18 month list for a 17-month-old or any child who could use the slower pace.

17-20 Months Resources

Weekly Checklist

Curriculum	This Week	Check It Off!
Guide		
Active Baby, Healthy Brain	daily	☐ ☐ ☐ ☐
Language Arts		
Reading	daily	☐ ☐ ☐ ☐
Flower Whistle	twice a week	☐ ☐
Math		
Junior Rainbow Pebbles	twice a week	☐ ☐
STEM		
Match the Buddies	twice a week	☐ ☐
Faces Puzzles	once a week	☐
Baby Popi	once a week	☐
SmartMax Baby STEM	twice a week	☐ ☐
PlanToys Stacking Rocket	once a week	☐
Emotional Intelligence		
Bébé Doll	twice a week	☐ ☐
Playmobil Community	twice a week	☐ ☐
Nins Neighborhood	twice a week	☐ ☐
Motor Skills		
Pat-A-Cake (scheduled with reading)	once a week	☐
Gymnic Over Ball	3 times a week	☐ ☐ ☐

18-24 Months Active Baby, Healthy Brain

Weekly Checklist

Massage

	Mon.	Tues.	Wed.	Thurs.	Fri.
Massage (working up to crocodile position)					

Motor Planning

	Mon.	Tues.	Wed.	Thurs.	Fri.
Animal movements with starts and stops					
Dancing with 2-3 actions					
Moving while singing / talking					

Upper Body

	Mon.	Tues.	Wed.	Thurs.	Fri.
Hanging from a bar or rings					
Climbing furniture					
Wheelbarrows					

Vestibular Stimulation

	Mon.	Tues.	Wed.	Thurs.	Fri.
Leg hugs					
Spinning and body parts					
Trapeze bar					
Wheelbarrow on ramps or beams					
Swinging and spinning					
Kicking with one foot					
Steps / stairs					
Rolling on a large ball					
Walk on wobbly board					

Music, Rhythm, and Song

	Mon.	Tues.	Wed.	Thurs.	Fri.
Rhythm activity (such as maracas to music)					
Copy rhythm patterns					
Rhyming movement / songs with actions					

Vision

	Mon.	Tues.	Wed.	Thurs.	Fri.
Visual tracking with rolling games (rolling balls, ping pong balls in a hoop, in and out of tubes)					
Cover one eye while tracking					
Flashlight tracking without moving head					
Reading books / special scrapbook					
Pretending / imitation / dress-up					

Vestibular Stimulation

	Mon.	Tues.	Wed.	Thurs.	Fri.
Water play					
Balloon throw & catch or beanbag hand to hand					
Rolling balls & running to catch					
Hitting balloons with a fly swatter					
Standing to throw small ball					
Hoops (sit & raise, walk around, backwards, rock in and out, step in and out, jump in)					
Colorful ribbons (walk, heel to toe, one foot either side, sideways, jump along, tiger crawl, bear walk)					

21-24 Months
A Funny and Opinionated Little Person

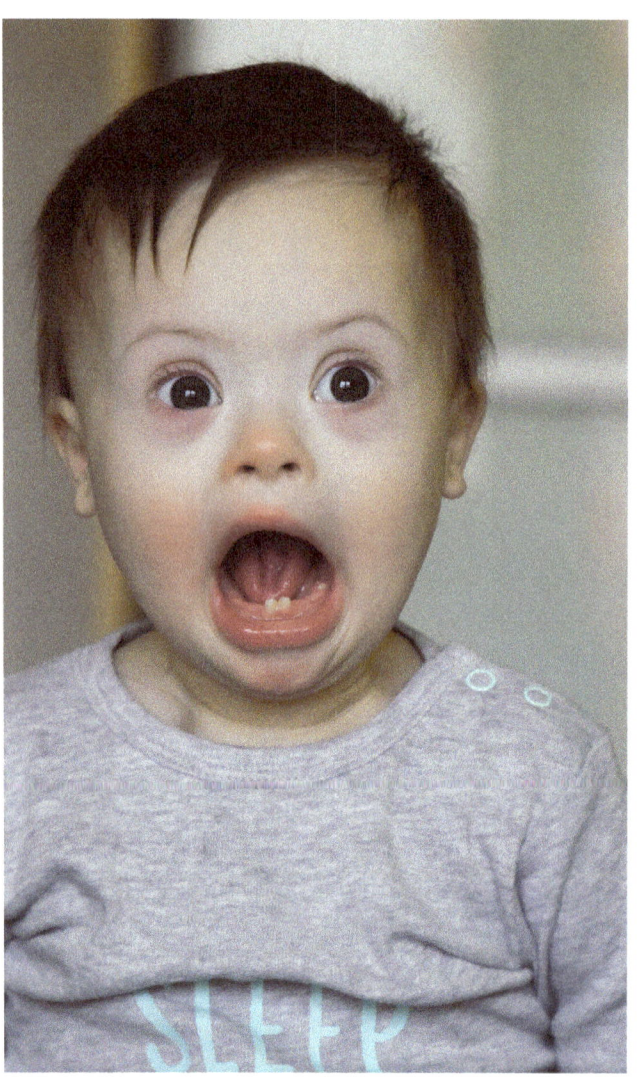

Mastering Communication

The biggest emphasis of these months will continue to be communication. Use sign language, verbal communication, or both to help your child communicate! As your child gains words, you gain insight into his amazing and funny personality. This age is beyond phenomenal, and you're going to love hearing what's going through his head!

Side note: you're going to hear a lot of "NO!" around your house. Your child loves being able to make his own choices now and won't hesitate to make his opinion known. To minimize stress, work at asking him only if you are ready for his answer. Don't ask, "Can I buckle you up before we leave?" if you must leave this minute and will be buckling him regardless of his answer. It would be better to tell him, "I need to buckle you up now. Would you like to hold the car or the doll while we're driving?" That lets him have control over what he can have control over, and it leaves you asking when you're asking and telling/directing when the choice is strictly yours.

Reading

As always, your toddler will continue to benefit from daily reading time. As mentioned before, reading increases auditory processing skills, visual perception, language development, connection, and so much more. Read a book from your kit, the library, or your bookshelf—just make sure you're reading together.

Case #1: Ember

If you look up firecracker in the dictionary, you'll probably find a picture of Ember. She loves to push, pull, run, dance, and do anything physical. She spins endlessly, runs full steam ahead into things, and climbs and jumps off of everything. She chews on anything she can get her hands on, is a huge fan of loud noises, and touches everything.

Busy Ember has another type of sensory processing disorder, known as sensory seeking. She doesn't know where she is in space unless she's moving, and she needs intense physical input to calm and regulate her body and to help her know where she is in space. As you suspect, we'd highly recommend an assessment with an occupational therapist and integration of the OT's plan into everyday life. You may be shocked at what she can accomplish once her sensory system isn't yelling at her all day long!

Getting her to sit down for any of the STEM skills may be tough. You could try setting the pieces across the room and have her run and grab one, then run back, slamming into a giant beanbag before placing the piece where it belongs. That may regulate her brain enough to be able to think more clearly. Try moving quiet activities, like reading, to immediately after challenging physical activities, such as *Active Baby, Healthy Brain* exercises.

Ember may be your most challenging student this year, but the rewards will pay off as you help her bring her body into balance and channel some of her untapped energy.

Case #2: Owen

When Owen was born, you were shocked to learn that he had Down Syndrome. Two years later, you are still deeply in love with him, and are so familiar with his routines that you rarely think of his diagnosis. However, there are some delays that Owen works with every day. His low muscle tone makes it hard for him to walk or talk. His motor skills are at about the level of a 14-month-old, as are his verbal skills. However, his comprehension is at age level, and he loves all things that move.

For Owen, you're going to want to move to the most appropriate activities for him, which may primarily be the 13- to 16-month list. You'll also want to really emphasize sign language to give him the communication he so desperately needs. As he continues to grow and develop, it's going to be most helpful if you walk through the tools at whatever pace he needs. You may find he hits growth spurts and suddenly is ready for activities for a 20-month-old, or, even more likely, that he is ready for age-appropriate social / emotional skills but lags a bit in motor skills. Just let him enjoy life at his pace, and be ready to provide the next level up for him when he gets there. Chances are, he'll be there soon!

Case #3: Faith

Since birth Faith has been a very visual learner, and it didn't take long for her to become a great little conversationalist as well. She shares your love for books and seemed extraordinarily interested in learning to read.

Being an advocate for early education, you made her sight word flashcards, which she loves. She read for the first time at 16 months, and now at 22 months she absolutely loves to read. Most people are skeptical of her skills until they actually see her in action.

First off, this is amazing! How impressive that you cultivated her interest and developed a very real skill so early!

Second, you are going to want to make sure that you continue to fuel her delight instead of quenching the flame. Take the time to ask yourself if the activities you select are in any way crushing her spirit, but don't let that fear keep you from capitalizing on her strength.

For her chart, you'll want to add in *All About Reading, 100 Easy Lessons*, or *The Reading Lesson*. Yes, it's unheard of. Yes, you're going to get some side-eye for this at the next homeschool group meeting. However, it is what Faith is ready for, and of all the experts in the world, you're hers! Compare sample pages, complete any placement tests with her, then put her at the appropriate level. Of course, she won't be able to do the fine motor portions of the work, but she's going to love the reading.

We'll keep the rest of her chart standard. We don't want her to abandon all other skills while she chases this one, but we do want to encourage her in the area in which she is gifted.

P.S. This is the actual story of one of the original Timberdoodle kids, though it was before *All About Reading* existed. And yes, she still loves reading!

21-24 Months Resources

Weekly Checklist

Curriculum	This Week	Check It Off!
Guide		
Active Baby, Healthy Brain	daily	☐ ☐ ☐ ☐ ☐
Language Arts		
Reading	daily	☐ ☐ ☐ ☐ ☐
Flower Whistle	twice a week	☐ ☐
Math		
Junior Rainbow Pebbles	twice a week	☐ ☐
STEM		
Match the Buddies	twice a week	☐ ☐
Faces Puzzles	once a week	☐
Baby Popi	once a week	☐
SmartMax Baby STEM	twice a week	☐ ☐
PlanToys Stacking Rocket	once a week	☐
Emotional Intelligence		
Bébé Doll	twice a week	☐ ☐
Playmobil Community	twice a week	☐ ☐
Nins Neighborhood	twice a week	☐ ☐
Motor Skills		
Pat-A-Cake (scheduled with reading)	once a week	☐
Gymnic Over Ball	3 times a week	☐ ☐ ☐

18-24 Months Active Baby, Healthy Brain

Weekly Checklist

Massage

	Mon.	Tues.	Wed.	Thurs.	Fri.
Massage (working up to crocodile position)					

Motor Planning

	Mon.	Tues.	Wed.	Thurs.	Fri.
Animal movements with starts and stops					
Dancing with 2-3 actions					
Moving while singing / talking					

Upper Body

	Mon.	Tues.	Wed.	Thurs.	Fri.
Hanging from a bar or rings					
Climbing furniture					
Wheelbarrows					

Vestibular Stimulation

	Mon.	Tues.	Wed.	Thurs.	Fri.
Leg hugs					
Spinning and body parts					
Trapeze bar					
Wheelbarrow on ramps or beams					
Swinging and spinning					
Kicking with one foot					
Steps / stairs					
Rolling on a large ball					
Walk on wobbly board					

Music, Rhythm, and Song

	Mon.	Tues.	Wed.	Thurs.	Fri.
Rhythm activity (such as maracas to music)					
Copy rhythm patterns					
Rhyming movement / songs with actions					

Vision

	Mon.	Tues.	Wed.	Thurs.	Fri.
Visual tracking with rolling games (rolling balls, ping pong balls in a hoop, in and out of tubes)					
Cover one eye while tracking					
Flashlight tracking without moving head					
Reading books / special scrapbook					
Pretending / imitation / dress-up					

Vestibular Stimulation

	Mon.	Tues.	Wed.	Thurs.	Fri.
Water play					
Balloon throw & catch or beanbag hand to hand					
Rolling balls & running to catch					
Hitting balloons with a fly swatter					
Standing to throw small ball					
Hoops (sit & raise, walk around, backwards, rock in and out, step in and out, jump in)					
Colorful ribbons (walk, heel to toe, one foot either side, sideways, jump along, tiger crawl, bear walk)					

Item-by-Item Introductions

Active Baby, Healthy Brain

A Guide Like No Other

Babies crave more than just a meal and a cuddle. They are eager, voracious learners. Many new parents are just as enthusiastic to start homeschooling their babies, but they don't know where to start.

Active Baby, Healthy Brain is the most practical handbook for parents who are enthralled with every aspect of their baby's intellectual and physical development. It is simple and to the point, with ideas that are quick and easy to implement. Each activity is presented with detailed, step-by-step instructions, and the appealing illustrations help to make everything crystal clear.

Active Baby, Healthy Brain

Infant | Toddler | Birth to 2 Kit

Once your baby is safely home, you will want to do more than just feed him and keep him warm. You'll want to begin to interact and build relationship. However, you'll also want to make this easy to implement since you're running on what is likely the least sleep of your life.

Active Baby, Healthy Brain will do the trick. It is packed with information and ideas to help you get to know your little one better. It will also show you how to help him grow and develop in a balanced manner, making the most of his amazing brain. You're going to have a blast!

And while the overall tone is one of having fun with your baby, the author makes sure you understand the crucial connections between the activities and the development of your baby's body and brain.

No single activity takes more than 2 minutes, and all that's required is 10 minutes a day. Yet when we tried to implement the daily instructions with our foster babies, we found it hard to remember what exactly we were supposed to do each day.

The lists on the preceding pages of this handbook are not designed to replace the book in any way. (Our notes are cryptic at best, and you will definitely need the often-illustrated instructions in the book itself.) But after familiarizing yourself with this season's activities, just use the checklists to make sure you're not forgetting any activities this week. (These are the *Active Baby, Healthy Brain* checklists above, in the Weekly Checklists Age-by-Age section.)

Caution

It is vital that you never allow your baby's head to flop—always support the head and neck. Modify or skip the activity if your baby is not yet strong enough to support himself with ease. For those of you with preemies or babies with special needs, take into account adjusted age and current ability. This program is designed to be ability-based, not age-dictated, so work through it at your child's pace.

Scheduling

Unless otherwise noted, you'll want to do each activity 1-3 times a day at most. (The one exception is massage—work that into your baby's day just as often as you can. The sensory integration is priceless!) Since most activities take 30 seconds or less, this is definitely not as time-intensive as you might think at first glance!

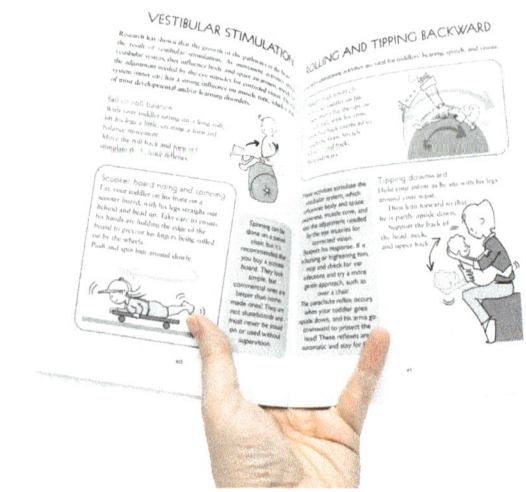

Language Arts

Three Tips on Language Development

Stop for a moment and marvel at the comprehension needed for your little one to follow simple directions, ask for a favorite snack, or even express his delight in seeing his mother.

The number-one thing you can do for language development is to talk with your child. You'll be astonished at how much of your vocabulary he can quote by age 2!

The second is just as achievable—read together. Reading develops vocabulary in great part because it provides a structured way to talk with your child about things you may not otherwise discuss.

Third, sign language is a truly remarkable tool—use it! Your child will be able to communicate with you long before he figures out how to make his mouth work as he wants.

What's the bottom line? It's the same tool with 3 different techniques.

Talk—it's going to make all the difference!

Visual Perception Collection

Infant | ~~Toddler~~ | Birth to 2 Kit

This charming collection of board books will be an excellent tool for stimulating your baby's mind. Black-and-white images have the strongest impact on your baby at birth.

The Visual Perception Collection uses skillfully designed high-contrast, black-and-white illustrations—perfect for baby's developing eyesight. However, starting at around 3 months, the baby's ability to see color improves. As a bonus, every page in this series also includes a splash of additional color. That extra pop of color means this is a series that will grow with your baby.

The Visual Perception Collection can also be the perfect tummy-time books for your newborn. Without tummy time, your baby may experience delays in developing the crucial motor skills of learning to push up, roll over, and crawl. But when it comes time to be on their bellies, most babies fuss. We also like using these books to reduce a baby's boredom and unhappiness during tummy time. The high-contrast shapes and patterns in the Visual Perception Collection provide the baby with something simple and engaging to focus on.

The Visual Perception Collection includes 3 board books. The first, *Hello,* is about engaging with friends, family, and soft, fluffy toys. The second book, *Animals,* introduces your baby to a variety of creatures. Finally, *Outdoors* sparks discussion of summer flowers, winter snow, and rainy sidewalk puddles. Each title has sturdy holes for your baby to peek through, adding another layer of engagement to his reading experience.

Scheduling

Use this in baby's early days to make tummy time more enjoyable, for reading time, or both!

Indestructibles Set of 3

Infant | ~~Toddler~~ | Birth to 2 Kit

Parents of infants have enough to worry about without trying to safeguard their baby's reading material. Chew-proof, rip-proof, and nontoxic, *Indestructibles* are built for the way babies read!

Made of incredible paper-like material for your baby to hold, grab, chew, pull, and bend, *Indestructibles* can handle it all. Bright and swirling with color, these wordless books allow parents' stories to be as rich as the artwork.

And for those inevitable encounters with food or its by-products, parents will be relieved to know they can just toss an *Indestructible* book into the wash.

Scheduling

Give your little one free access to these books while teething. As he gets older, use the illustrations of these wordless books to inspire your creative and impromptu stories.

L Is for Lion

Infant | ~~Toddler~~ | Birth to 2 Kit

Introduce your little ones to the fascinating world of animals with *L Is for Lion*, an extraordinary touch-and-feel animal alphabet book designed to delight their senses. Showcasing a diverse array of creatures, what sets this book apart is the sensory experience it offers. Every 2-page spread provides a unique tactile adventure for your baby's tiny hands, from flamingos' feathery softness to koalas' furry ears. Watch your child's eyes light up as he explores the amusing animal illustrations and experiences the different textures. *L Is for Lion* isn't just an alphabet book; it's a multisensory exploration that will captivate your child's imagination and create treasured moments of discovery. *L Is for Lion* is the perfect addition to your little one's early learning library, offering an engaging and interactive way to introduce him to the fascinating world of letters and animals.

Scheduling

Use as a fantastic resource for your everyday reading time with your baby. At first, your little one will enjoy the vibrant pictures, and as he gets more interactive, he'll enjoy exploring the textures. The alphabet connection makes this an even more multifaceted resource to grow with your little one into his preschool years!

My First Touch and Feel Cards

Infant | ~~Toddler~~ | Birth to 2 Kit

Flashcards for babies? We did that in the 1980s. Surely in 40 years something better must have been designed. It has! *My First Touch and Feel Cards* are classic educational flashcards but souped up for today's babies.

Each set includes 16 sturdy hardboard cards, suitably thick to withstand clumsy small hands and coated with a wipe-clean covering. Every beautifully designed photo depicts the name of an everyday item and includes a textured portion—fluffy, bumpy, or fuzzy—for your baby to touch, perfect to encourage sensory processing.

However, it is the back of the card that makes the *My First Touch and Feel Cards* an educational treasure chest. Expertly designed to enhance early language development, on the back of each card is a host of questions for parents to ask from the obvious to the creative. For parents who find themselves asking only "What is this?" questions, the prompts on the back of the *My First Touch and Feel Cards* allow for more open-ended questions.

Plus, each box includes ideas on how to use the flashcards, including simple games to play. Excellent for helping young children develop their verbal skills and vocabulary, *My First Touch and Feel Cards* are a fantastic resource for homeschooling families. The card decks each come in a robust cardboard box with a velcro closure.

Scheduling

As soon as baby is sitting up, he'll likely find these cards fascinating. We'd suggest doing some every day, stopping while it's still fun. Typically, you'll start with Animals and then swap / add First Words when baby is ready for some variety.

Baby Sign Language Cards

Infant | ~~Toddler~~ | Birth to 2 Kit

Are you parenting an infant or nurturing a precocious toddler with an appetite for learning, or have you been blessed with a child who defies typical verbal development? The National Institutes of Health found that signing babies talk sooner, have stronger parent/child bonds with less frustration and crying, and engage in more sophisticated play.

Baby Sign Language Flash Cards is a very accessible resource for learning and teaching American Sign Language. Using symbolic gestures, *Baby Sign Language* features clear, brightly colored photographs of 50 of the most valuable ASL signs your family will need. On the reverse of each card are easy-to-understand photos and descriptions that show you how each sign is done. The cards are laminated and sturdy, and the signs are easy to follow.

Babies learn fastest when sign language is included in a variety of daily routines and fun activities. So place cards on your fridge, in a corner of the bathroom mirror, or on the changing table for quick and easy reference.

Baby Sign Language Flash Cards are not intended to be a primary sign language resource for parents but rather a fun activity to enjoy together. However, if used consistently, baby sign language will provide an enjoyable way to sign about things your baby is interested in. Don't forget to read the included practical quick-start guide!

Scheduling

Introduce these when your baby is ready, often around 6-8 months. As he approaches age 1, expect him to become increasingly interested in mastering and using these signs. Once you hit that stage, we'd suggest really focusing in on 2 new signs each week.

Baby Babble Collection

~~Infant~~ | Toddler | Birth to 2 Kit

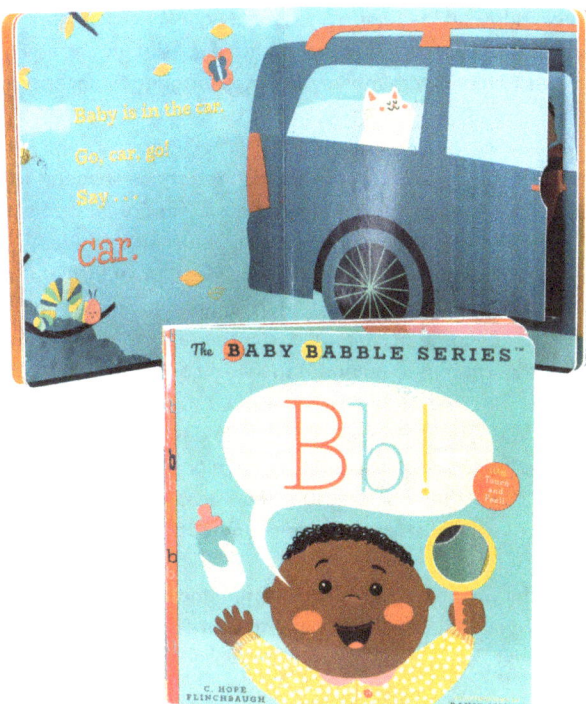

How can parents help their tiny talker go from baby babble to understandable words? The Baby Babble Series! This collection of 2 board books will encourage babies to use their first sounds as building blocks for their growing vocabulary.

Baby Babble Series was designed to help babies and toddlers progress from babbling to talking by focusing on different fundamental sounds that babies find easy to pronounce.

The interactive Baby Babble Series invites babies to touch and feel textured material, like a soft kitty or a felt blanket, as they explore and practice new words.

The illustrations are bright and engaging, and the storyline is perfect for this age group.

Scheduling

This series will star as part of your daily reading time.

Ditty Bird Collection

~~Infant~~ | Toddler | Birth to 2 Kit

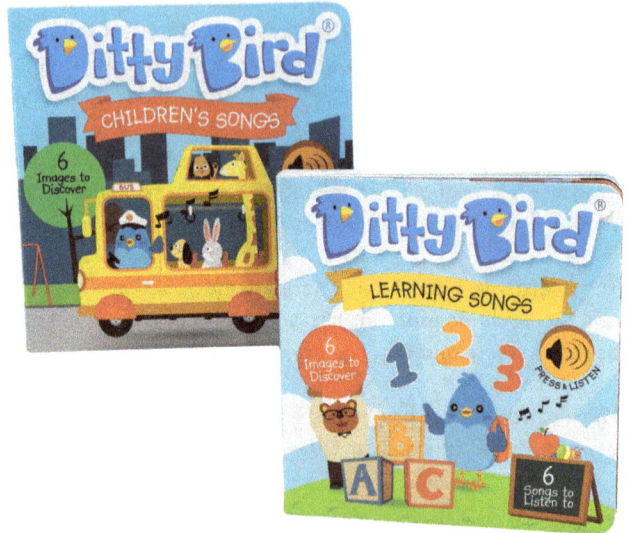

Babies utilize all their senses to learn. So it should be no surprise that research has shown that exposing your baby to music can help him master complex language concepts faster.

Even before babies can talk, they can react and respond to music. That is why Ditty Bird books are essential for babies' learning and development. While any book that includes sounds can help with sensory development, Ditty Bird books—which utilize rhymes, cadence, and music—will help your baby become accustomed to a range of sounds, which is essential for him to navigate the world as he grows.

Ditty Bird books have been specifically designed to promote language skills, auditory development, and music appreciation. Each book features curved corners for safety; bright, colorful illustrations; and sound buttons.

Your baby will be encouraged to listen and sing along as Ditty Bird introduces him to easy-to-learn songs. The sound dot on every page is effortlessly activated by a tiny finger.

Each book comes with a longlasting battery, but if needed, the batteries are easy to replace with full instructions on the back.

Scheduling

Make this book part of your reading time. You'll cover introductory music, cause and effect, and so much more!

A to Z: An Alphabet of Animals

~~Infant~~ | Toddler | Birth to 2 Kit

We have found that using books for teaching the alphabet is helpful for little ones and easy for parents. Alphabet books are a great way to introduce toddlers to reading by helping them to associate letters with objects and sounds. Alphabet books for early listeners will help your toddlers build their vocabulary, so they are an excellent choice for children moving from infancy into toddlerhood.

Colorful and exciting, A *to Z: An Alphabet of Animals* introduces children to letter fun without making learning seem boring. Animals are cleverly disguised by the shape of the letters, and toddlers lift the flaps to discover which ones are hiding under each letter.

The chunky pages are toddler friendly, and the thick flaps are easy for chubby fingers to lift, though as prone to tear as all flaps. Young listeners will meet a narwhal under the *N*, an owl under the *O*, and a peacock under the *P*.

The love of literacy begins with little ones listening to the reading of simple books. *A to Z: An Alphabet of Animals* allows toddlers to become familiar with letters in a fun and relaxed atmosphere.

Scheduling

What a fun way to add more interaction to your daily reading time! Work it in as often as you'd like.

My First Peter and the Wolf

~~Infant~~ | Toddler | Birth to 2 Kit

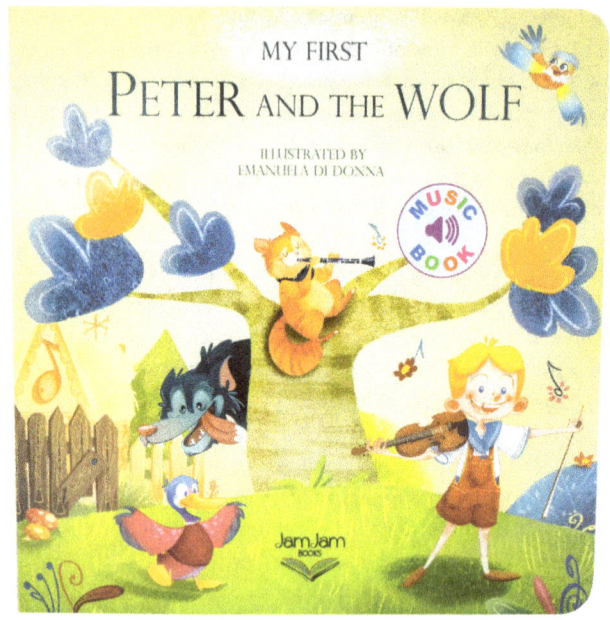

Child prodigy Sergei Prokofiev was born in 1891 in a village in Ukraine. He began composing music when he was just 5. Given this, it should be no surprise that one of his most beloved pieces, *Peter and the Wolf*, was written as a child's introduction to the orchestra. Each character in the story is represented by a different instrument or group of instruments.

My First Peter and The Wolf will introduce your toddler to the classic tale of how a little boy outsmarts a big, bad wolf. Are you familiar with the original storyline? In that case, you will be relieved to know that while *My First Peter and The Wolf* follows the basic narrative, this version is more toddler-friendly. No duck dinner for the wolf!

The full-orchestra musical clips sound lovely, and your toddler will enjoy activating the sensors located on the sturdy pages. Just touch the sensor and enjoy the music. There are 6 high-quality sound segments, each 20-40 seconds long. The illustrations are well-matched to the story and will provide you with lots of discussion points. The final spread shows each of the main characters with the instruments that represented them. What a memorable way to introduce musical instruments to young children!

Scheduling

What a fun, musical addition to your daily reading time! Use as often as desired.

My First Words around the Home

~~Infant~~ | Toddler | Birth to 2 Kit

Tap into your little one's natural curiosity and give him the words he will need for the things he sees at home and in the backyard with *First Words around the Home*.

From the kitchen to the living room to the bedroom and the bathroom, there are well over 100 words for your baby to discover with *First Words around the Home*. In this exciting tour around the house, there are drawings of familiar objects and some not so familiar, like a vinyl record player and a pre-smartphone camera.

However, learning vocabulary words is just the beginning. In each scene, there are questions that guide parents in introducing their baby to counting, colors, comparison, and so much more. And as a special treat, a tiny mouse that your baby will love searching for is hiding on each spread.

Scheduling

Incorporate this book and its helpful questions into your daily reading time. Can you help your baby answer a different question each time you read?

100 First Words: Nature

~~Infant~~ | Toddler | Birth to 2 Kit

Get ready for an adventure in nature with *100 First Words: Nature*! This charming book is bursting with objects for little explorers to discover, and it features bold, easy-to-lift card flaps. Bright illustrations adorn each page, bringing the wonders of nature to life.

With flaps to lift on every page, kids will love diving into *100 First Words: Nature* repeatedly. Encouraging curiosity and engagement, this is the perfect addition to any young learner's library. It's more than just a book; it's a gateway to a lifelong love of nature and learning. With delightful artwork and interactive flaps, *100 First Words: Nature* introduces children to flowers, animals, and more in a very entertaining and educational way. Let the exploration begin!

Some weeks you might focus on a single spread; other times you might pick out 1 or 2 words on each page. As your little one's comprehension grows, ask him questions, such as "Who has spots?" or "Can you find the animal that hops?"

Scheduling
Read to your baby from this book once a week or as desired.

Flower Whistle

~~Infant~~ | Toddler | Birth to 2 Kit

Help your baby develop tongue, cheek, jaw, and lip muscles, as well as respiratory control for speech and feeding skills with the colorful Flower Whistle. With the sound providing instant positive reinforcement, the Flower Whistle is simple enough for babies as young as 3 months old to use. Both inhaling and exhaling through the Flower Whistle results in a baby-friendly sound. Noise of all kinds provides essential stimulation for brain development.

Made from soft material with no sharp metal mouth plates or screws, the Flower Whistle is also safe for your baby to chew. What a well-designed multisensory experience! Created by the people of Japan, this educational toy is finally an option for families in the U.S. In fact, the Flower Whistle is so new to the U.S. that your whistle may come in Japanese packaging!

Scheduling

Introduce this whistle as soon as your baby can grasp toys of this size. Initially he will likely use it as a teether, but as soon as he shows interest, demonstrate how to use it as a whistle. By the time he's walking, he will likely be quite proficient in whistle use!

Mathematics

A Fundamental Skill

You'll naturally count things with your toddler, from the number of times he can catch his ball to the number of figures in his Nins Neighborhood. Try making it a point to count something together every day, and your tiny tot will stay curious about numbers and eager to learn more!

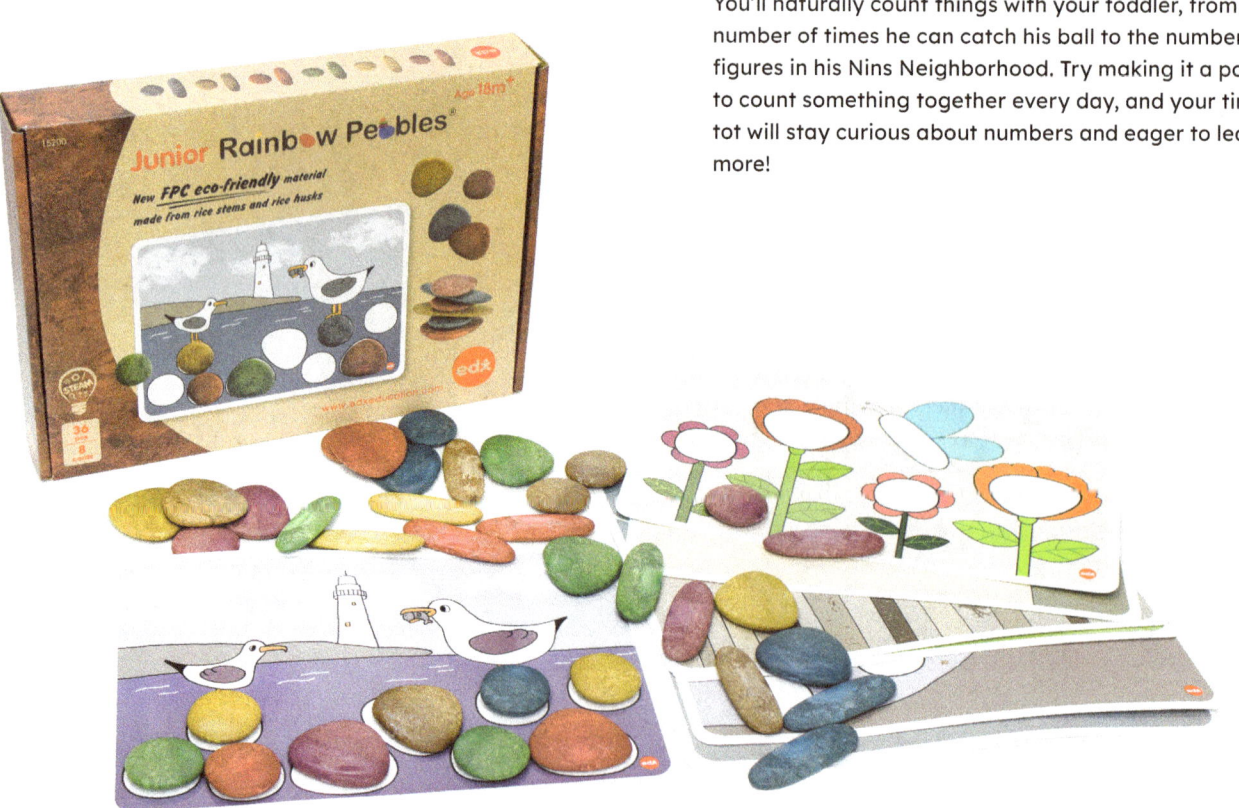

Junior Rainbow Pebbles

~~Infant~~ | Toddler | Birth to 2 Kit

As odd as it sounds, research indicates that early math skills are a better predictor of academic success than early reading skills. Junior Rainbow Pebbles makes math accessible to toddlers as young as 18 months.

Sort, stack, and sequence by size with these pleasing smooth, rubbery pebbles. Perfect for developing fine motor skills and creative design, Junior Rainbow Pebbles includes 36 pebbles in 3 shapes and 6 colors, as well as 8 large activity cards to create toddler-friendly building structures, patterns, and pictures.

The pebbles in this set are made from eco-friendly rice stems and husks and come in lovely muted shades of blue, green, brown, red, and purple. The 8 large, double-sided, laminated activity cards expound on this tranquil theme with pictures of autumn leaves and seashore activities.

Scheduling

This is a tool you likely won't use as designed before baby is 18 months old. When he's ready, add to your schedule about twice a week.

That said, if you have a younger toddler who is interested, you could start by just letting him manipulate the pieces. Do you have an empty tissue box that he could plop them into?

Next he can sort by color and eventually shape. To make sorting easier, either limit the pieces you give him or begin by having him hand you pieces to sort until you're down to the last a or 2. As his skills increase, he can do more and more.

Next, show him how to stack the Rainbow Pebbles. Because they are uneven, building will be a challenge, but the grippy surfaces will help him as he works to develop his fine motor skills.

Finally, introduce him to the activity cards, which will offer him opportunities to match colors and shapes and even present a building challenge or two. Such fun! Again, you can simplify initially by giving him only the pieces he needs and gradually scale up until he can find them himself.

STEM Learning

STEM Is Everywhere!

STEM learning is more than robotics and computer programming. STEM tools also include those that engage students in exploratory learning, discovery, and problem-solving. All these teach the foundational skills of critical thinking and short-term and long-term planning.

STEM includes your Junior Rainbow Pebbles as well as your Nins Neighborhood and your Peek & Pull Baby Tissue Box, even though they are listed elsewhere in this handbook. In assembling this guide, many of our products could easily have been classified as STEM, but the following tools seem especially appropriate for this category.

Sensory Spinners

Infant | ~~Toddler~~ | Birth to 2 Kit

New from Tiger Tribe, a design-led Australian brand, come Sensory Spinners—an engaging 3-piece baby toy to touch, explore, shake (makes a rattling sound), chew, and spin! Babies put everything in their mouths. However, when you want them to learn cause and effect or work on fine-motor skills, you need a toy that encourages their hands without traveling to their mouths. The colorful Sensory Spinners, with a large suction cup on the back, enable just that. Featuring a trio of cute Aussie animals, the Sensory Spinners spin freely with just a bump from a chubby hand and keep turning for a remarkably long time.

Your child's grasp of cause and effect will blossom as he engages with the Sensory Spinners. Once he tires of spinning them, simply release the suction for an auditory sensory delight, enabling him to shake each spinner for a gentle rattle sound. The spinners are designed with safety in mind, so he can freely explore, touch, and even teethe on the distinctive contours and textures of the cockatoo, koala, or wombat spinners.

Are you a family that is often on the go? Then you will be happy to know that the Sensory Spinners stick to restaurant tables, airplane windows, hotel tubs, Grandma's fridge, and just about anything with a smooth surface. They are an excellent distraction for a fussy toddler.

After a bit of in-house research, our team discovered that these Sensory Spinners outperformed others we tested in terms of spinning capability. Additionally, babies responded more to the animal-themed spinners than to those lacking distinct features like eyes to captivate their attention.

Scheduling

Infancy
Some babies will begin to handle, chew, and manipulate Sensory Spinners at this age, but most won't quite be ready.

6–18 Months
This is when Sensory Spinners get pretty amazing. Suction them onto the table, floor, or glass door and encourage baby to bat at them as often as you like.

Older Toddlers
As baby gets older, these become less of an everyday thing and more of a tucked-in-the-diaper-bag-for-emergencies tool. Use them in restaurants or doctor's offices for a novel and quiet toy.

Happy World Fruit Delivery

<mark>Infant</mark> | ~~Toddler~~ | <mark>Birth to 2 Kit</mark>

We are thrilled to introduce Happy World Fruit Delivery, a product designed to ignite curiosity and stimulate both sides of your baby's brain. The magnetic, high-contrast black-and-white blocks support your baby's developing eyesight. These versatile cubes feature captivating patterns on every side, providing endless interactive play and image-building opportunities. With Happy World Fruit Delivery, your newborn's tummy time will be engaging and happy, helping him during this crucial developmental activity.

The patented magnetic track cubes allow for ultimate versatility and creativity. The magnets rotate inside each block, ensuring that they snap together seamlessly, regardless of orientation. Each set includes 9 track cubes and 10 double-sided cards. One side features assembly challenges, while the other presents familiar black-and-white images. As your baby's color vision improves around 3 months, some cards introduce a splash of additional color, ensuring the cards grow with him.

Happy World Fruit Delivery is not just for infants but also for young children who are ready to explore the STEM aspects of learning. Thanks to the patented magnetic connection system that guarantees smooth attraction without polarity conflict, even the youngest learners can successfully build with these frustration-free blocks. The audible click when the blocks connect provides a delightful auditory experience for little ears.

Toddlers can also delve into stacking and basic construction skills with Happy World Fruit Delivery. A bonus fruit truck set enhances play by transporting fruit tiles along the tracks, offering endless possibilities for imaginative play and exploration.

Happy World Fruit Delivery exceeds international safety standards for infant products, promoting tactile and sensory development while offering years of enjoyment. Each block can be interconnected, encouraging toddlers to think creatively and unleash their imagination.

Qbi, the maker of Happy World Fruit Delivery, is dedicated to offering top-quality products that foster your child's development. Their safe and educational toys promote creativity and imagination, encouraging your child's growth and exploration. The Qbi kits have received full authentication from US STEM.org, guaranteeing they adhere to strict educational standards. With diverse attachment options and track patterns, Happy World Fruit Delivery ensures your little one hours of entertainment and learning.

Scheduling

Happy World Fruit Delivery is one of those amazing resources that will grow with your child's development. As your baby learns new skills, he will use this set in different ways. We suggest putting it on your schedule twice weekly so it doesn't slip your mind but playing with it more frequently if desired.

0-6 Months

For a few months, the primary use of Happy World Fruit Delivery is to stimulate your baby's visual perception. You can place the cards or a block structure on the floor for tummy time or set up anywhere he can benefit from visual stimulation.

6-24 Months

Once your baby's grasping and sitting skills take off, Happy World Fruit Delivery will offer a whole new range of play. Your child will enjoy pulling down the structures you have created. He will also quickly discover that the pieces are magnetically attracted and enjoy experimenting with putting them together. Over time, your child will be able to build towers and put pieces together into structures. Happy World Fruit Delivery is a motivating way for your child to practice his motor skills, and he will be mesmerized as you set the delivery truck in motion and appreciate stories of the fruit deliveries it completes. The discovery of cause and effect, together with stacking and building, makes Happy World Fruit Delivery a great STEM resource.

Older Toddlers

As your little one grows, he can help you replicate the designs on the pattern side of the cards. Eventually, he'll be able to match them all on his own. Building them flat is the first step, but you can challenge older preschoolers to stack them vertically as they build. Replicating these assembly patterns is a wonderful introduction to translating from 2 dimensions to 3 dimensions.

Your child will also enjoy sending the fruit truck racing down the track. You can even create challenges by showing your child a "hungry" toy and asking him to build a road that the delivery truck can use to bring some fruit.

Match the Buddies

~~Infant~~ | Toddler | Birth to 2 Kit

It may be hard to believe that your little one who has barely learned to walk is ready to work on puzzles, but he is. With their uber-thick, extra-large puzzle pieces, Match the Buddies puzzles are a perfect introduction.

And the topic, buddies, is one that this age will find fascinating. I appreciate that the designer did not do mirror images of the buddies but included slight differences. This variation between similar yet distinctive animals can produce all sorts of fodder for conversation with budding linguists.

Match the Buddies puzzles will help develop your toddler's concentration, motor skills, language skills, and logical thinking.

Scheduling

Begin by handing your baby the matching piece and helping him push it into place. Fantastic!

Now can he do it by himself? Can he discern the right piece between 2 options? Continue to scaffold and increase the difficulty over the next months until he can do all the puzzles with minimal assistance.

Faces Puzzles

~~Infant~~ | Toddler | Birth to 2 Kit

Babies are drawn to faces, so what better subject matter for 1 of baby's first puzzles? Match the symmetrical face pieces to assemble 1 of 8 smiley faces.

The Faces Puzzles set features sturdy, high-quality, thick cardboard pieces necessary for this age group! With a distinctive color palette and whimsical art, Faces Puzzles are ideal for developing manual dexterity, visual perception, and logical thinking. Designed and manufactured in Europe from the finest materials, Faces Puzzles are made with nontoxic inks and with your baby's safety in mind. The small, travel-friendly box is perfect for on-the-go fun.

Scheduling

Babies as young as **12-18 months** may be ready to help you assemble these puzzles when you hand them both pieces and assist in sliding them together.

Over the next year, gradually help them learn to find the matching half and solve this puzzle on their own. While sifting through all the pieces may be too difficult for even a 2-year-old on his first try, it can be achieved by even your younger toddler with repeated, scaffolded practice.

As your toddler's skills develop, we suggest working on a puzzle as part of his daily routine 3-5 times a week. Choose any of the puzzles in our curriculum (including Wooden Pegging Game and Stacking Rocket) or rotate in your favorite family hand-me-downs.

Baby Popi

~~Infant~~ | Toddler | Birth to 2 Kit

Tap Baby Popi's 2 elegant little birds and 1 perky cat to see them bob. Push a bit harder and watch them leap out and away. Returning the wooden animals to their homes will encourage your baby's eye-hand coordination. Retrieving them after they have flown the coop will burn off a little pre-nap energy. Baby Popi's addition of characters on the end of each peg keeps them from rolling under the refrigerator. When your baby is old enough, have him match Baby Popi's colored pegs to the holes they belong in. Pop-up peg toys are classic additions to Montessori classrooms and are favored by physical therapists.

Scheduling

Some babies are gifted with great hand-eye coordination and will be interested in this months before their first birthday. For most little ones, though, we anticipate that they would begin to really enjoy it somewhere around 18 months old.

Your baby will probably learn to remove the pegs first. What a great game!

Next he'll either learn to drop them back into their holes or begin trying to bounce them out again. We suggest pulling this out at least once a week, but working with it for even 5 minutes at a time may be plenty for his attention span!

PlanToys Stacking Rocket

~~Infant~~ | Toddler | Birth to 2 Kit

By far one of the most attractive stacking toys we've found, PlanToy's Stacking Rocket is much more than a mere tower set. Each of the 4 rainbow-colored disks is a double-sided shape puzzle with a smaller piece inside. Even the cute little astronaut is a shape puzzle! This means that even before a toddler can figure out how to stack the rings, he will gain experience in solving some simple puzzles.

Crafted from recycled, preservative-free rubberwood and stained with organic color pigments and water-based natural dyes, Stacking Rocket encourages shape recognition (early math), colors, and stacking, and it will help develop your little one's fine motor skills and concentration.

The 11-piece Stacking Rocket includes 5 different shapes plus the rocket base. When your toddler has outgrown the Stacking Rocket, it will make a lovely addition to his bookshelves.

Scheduling

Your baby will first experiment with knocking the rocket over—yay, gravity!

Next, hand him 1 of the rings and its corresponding shape, and help him put the puzzle together. Soon he will be able to pick out the correct shape.

As that becomes easy, move to having him assemble more than 1 ring at a time, assisting him until he can assemble it all by himself. (This will take a long time, so be prepared to celebrate mini-successes!)

SmartMax Baby STEM

~~Infant~~ | Toddler | Birth to 2 Kit

When can you introduce a child to STEM? SmartMax Baby STEM allows even the earliest of learners to build successfully with this collection of multifaceted magnetic construction pieces for babies.

The powerful magnets are permanently encapsulated inside chunky, multicolored bars, which makes them safer and more accessible for babies.

SmartMax magnets can carry up to 60 times their weight, so designs stay together and come apart with a gentle tug.

This set includes long, short, and curved bars, plus plum-sized, lightweight balls just right for little hands to manipulate.

There are also 3 wobbly cars with happy drivers and a magnetic pull rope to convert the vehicles into a train. Plus, there are also 4 mix-and-match roly-poly citizens with magnetic personalities! SmartMax Baby STEM is a versatile, intellectually stimulating construction set that cleans up in a snap!

> Scheduling

The possibilities are endless. We suggest diving into the world of SmartMax with your child once a week after age 1.

0-10 Months

You won't use SmartMax Baby STEM as construction tools for a while, but right now you can use them as toys for your baby to pull apart and explore, or even as structures for him to knock down.

10-12 Months

As your baby gets more mobile, he will thoroughly enjoy knocking structures over and pulling pieces apart. But it won't be long now until he's building his own inventions.

12 Months and Up

Show him how pieces stick together and offer him suggestions for building designs.

Looking for a new idea? Here are some suggestions.

1. Bowling

Try knocking a tower over by bowling for it with his Over Ball.

2. Storytelling

Build a race car, a castle, a robot, or a boat and enjoy story time. Depending on your child's interest, the car could be carrying food for the hungry puppy or racing to get away from the cranky robot.

3. Colors

You can teach colors with SmartMax Baby STEM! When building a multicolored tower, talk about each piece's color. "Do you want the purple one?" "I'm going to put a green one on." Point out color similarities too. "This blue one is the same color as your shirt!"

4. Sorting by Color

Have your older toddler sort the blocks by color.

5. What Size Is It?

Now have him sort the blocks by size and by shape. This will be a perfect opportunity to introduce the vocabulary of *bigger* and *smaller*. This is a very practical place to use the vocabulary and familiarize your child with the concepts.

6. Count

Introduce counting by coaching your toddler to hand you 1 piece, 2 pieces, etc.

7. First, Second, Third

Work on other math vocabulary, such as, "Put this piece on second" or "Should we add a third piece?"

What else will you come up with?

Emotional Intelligence

A Crucial Life Skill

These 4 tools teach very different aspects of social interaction, which is why together they are invaluable. By reading and practicing the faces in *Making Faces*, your baby will be learning to identify and express emotions. The Peeka Mirror teaches self-awareness and imitation skills, in addition to many others. Bébé doll is amazing for teaching nurturing, recognition of the feelings of others, and fine motor skills. Playmobil Community and Nins Neigborhood introduce storytelling 101, empathy, humor, and more.

Making Faces: A First Book of Emotions

Infant | ~~Toddler~~ | Birth to 2 Kit

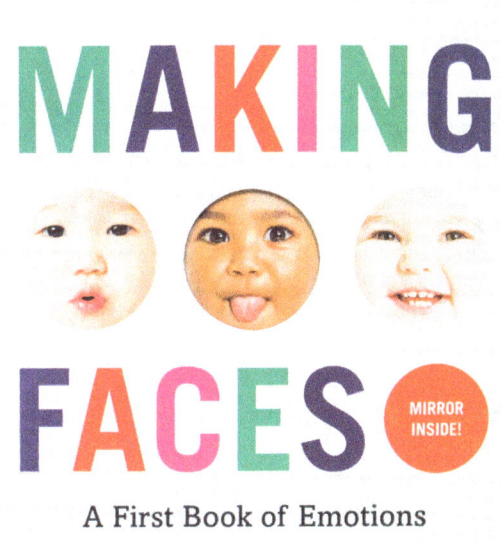

A simple introduction to 5 common emotions, *Making Faces: A First Book of Emotions* is a wonderfully interactive book for babies and toddlers. This beautiful board book presents the most familiar baby emotions: happy, sad, angry, surprised, and silly.

On the left-hand page, *Making Faces* uses large photographs of a single child's face on a white background to provide maximum contrast and to help babies zero in on facial expressions. On the opposite page, your baby is asked to find the same face among photos showing all 5 feelings. The last page in *Making Faces* includes a mirror where you and your baby can practice making your own faces.

Scheduling

For a tiny little one, just read the book as written and help baby point to the answers.

As he gets older, he will start pointing to the match on his own.

As soon as he masters that, start asking him to find a different face than the text suggests—for instance, on the "surprised" page, have him find a sad, happy, angry, or silly face.

And don't forget to use the mirror. It's so much fun to watch a baby master facial expressions!

Peeka Mirror

<mark>Infant</mark> | ~~Toddler~~ | <mark>Birth to 2 Kit</mark>

As your baby's vision begins to sharpen, he will love to look at faces—especially his own—which is a wonderful thing for his development.

Now with Peeka Mirror, your baby will have easy access to his reflection, along with a variety of exciting textures and colors for added visual stimulation. The Peeka Mirror's bumpy handles provide tactile input and are safe enough for teething. The multitextured silicone balls that slide along the top and bottom of the frame encourage cross-midline play and fine-motor skills. The easel back on the Peeka Mirror allows it to be used on floors and tabletops or held during car trips and diaper changes.

Developed by doctors and therapists, the clear, shatter-resistant Peeka Mirror is easy to transport in a purse or diaper bag. Made from BPA- and phthalate-free food-grade silicone, the Peeka Mirror will be an endless source of educational entertainment for your baby.

With Peeka Mirror you can boost your baby's hand-eye coordination, language, listening, and imitation skills.

Scheduling

You're going to want to use this early and often with your little one. Grab it for tummy time or set it by the changing table. He may also love it for car time, but do check to see if it's making him motion-sick or if the sunlight is reflecting off of it into his eyes.

Bébé Doll

~~Infant~~ | Toddler | Birth to 2 Kit

Empathy—recognizing the feelings of others and responding with care—is a very complex social-emotional skill for a toddler to develop. Corolle's Bébé doll is a perfect companion for practicing such skills by enacting and reenacting diverse scenarios. This doll will allow you to demonstrate to your child that others may have different feelings than he has and provides the opportunity to help him respond.

The ideal size for your child to rock and cradle, Bébé doll's soft body is posable like a real baby. The doll's face, arms, and legs are made of delicately vanilla-scented soft vinyl with eyes that open and close. Let Bébé join your child in the bath, pool, or ocean. Just leave Bébé to dry using the nifty tab on the back after water play.

Forty-year-old Corolle has a reputation for designing babies that are the right look, size, feel, and scent for little ones to love and cherish. Teach fine-motor skills, responsibility, nurturing, and caring with Corolle's Bébé doll.

Bébé doll is designed for ages 18 months and older, but our little ones have been intrigued by dolls before that age, so feel free to break it out sooner as desired.

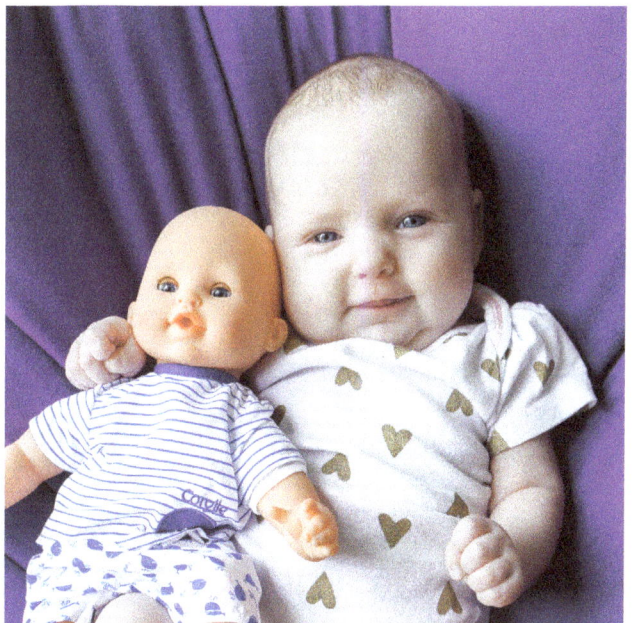

Scheduling

From about 8 months old, your baby can participate and mimic your actions as you care for Bébé doll. By 18 months old, your toddler can take the lead in soothing and bathing Bébé. Dressing and undressing Bébé doll, with help as needed, will practice the developmental skills necessary for your child to dress and undress himself. Be proactive in imitative play with Bébé doll at least 2 or more times a week, reenacting scenarios that a baby might experience.

Playmobil Community

~~Infant~~ | Toddler | Birth to 2 Kit

As a parent, you want to help your child develop the important skills that will benefit them for years to come. One way to do this is through engaging them in playing pretend. Pretend play can help your child develop their language skills, understand social and emotional scenarios, and learn how to problem-solve creatively.

That's where Playmobil Community comes in. With Playmobil Community, you can teach your child about turn-taking, problem-solving, emotional intelligence, empathy, and etiquette in a fun and interactive way. Plus, the diverse community members, vehicles, and settings can help your child learn about different people and things in the world around them, even as you build language and vocabulary. So why not start playing today?

Scheduling

To get started with Playmobil Community, we recommend setting aside time at least twice a week to play with your child.

1. Repeat and Complete Stories
The benefits of Playmobil Community stem from storytelling.

Simple, repetitive storylines are what this age group relishes. After your child has heard and seen you talk about the children going down the slide, he can begin to repeat and imitate parts of the story. You can ask your child questions like "Who wants to go down the slide now?" or "What does the girl want to do now?" to engage his language and storytelling skills.

2. Solve Problems

"Oh no, the boy's leg is hurt. Who can help?" The paramedic is ready to go! "The donut truck tipped over! Who can come to stop traffic and help?" The police officers are on their way! Playing through situations like these helps your child learn how people can help solve problems. At first, you will need to do all of the storytelling with Playmobil pieces, but soon, your child will start to mimic you for both the problems and the solutions.

3. Practice Emotional Intelligence and Empathy

Social scenarios dovetail with problem-solving. The donut truck driver may be worried, but he is happy after the emergency workers help him get on his way! One boy may be afraid of the cat, but his friend shows him it is friendly. As you play through various stories with your child, you can have the Playmobil characters cry, be happy, excited, surprised, and more. Imagining and resolving emotional scenarios is a good way for toddlers to practice empathy, much like reading fiction is helpful for older ages. It is also an intriguing way for them to experiment with feelings in a safe format.

4. Teach Etiquette

Along with building emotional intelligence, you can use Playmobil storytelling to practice simple etiquette. The basics of "please," "thank you," and "sorry" are an excellent place to start. The boy on the swing can say "sorry" for bumping into his sister, or the girl on the merry-go-round can say "thanks" to her friend for giving her a push.

5. Learn How to Take Turns

Your little one can practice turn-taking within the storyline as Playmobil people take turns on the slide or swing. He can also practice turn-taking in real life, as you and he take turns with different toys. Older siblings make excellent helpers for practicing sharing!

6. Discuss and Discern Likes vs. Dislikes

It's time to ride on the merry-go-round! This rider likes to go slow. Do you like to go slow or fast? Conversations like these may help you know your child's preferences, but his likes and dislikes can change quickly for a toddler. But what you are also developing is your toddler's important recognition that people are different and like different things.

7. Motor Skills and Thinking Skills

All of the Playmobil Community components encourage thinking skills and motor skills. The Donut Truck's features offer a special range of opportunities where your child can stack the donuts on the truck and load them in the trailer. The trailer's release on the back is a fun experiment in cause and effect. Working with these activities and helping the Playmobil characters stand up, sit down, and fit into other vehicles and sets will develop your child's motor and thinking skills.

8. Build Language and Vocabulary

Every element of Playmobil Community listed above helps to build your child's language and vocabulary. But it does even more! Beyond simple words like *truck*, *hat*, *drive*, *walk*, and so on, your stories can include color and prepositions (such as *above*, *below*, *behind*, and *in*). You can also familiarize your toddler with time words like *first*, *then*, and *finally* and adjectives like *fast* and *slow*. You've already incorporated words about emotions and maybe even abstract words like *brave* and *kind*. What a fun way to help your child's language skills blossom!

Nins Neighborhood

~~Infant~~ | **Toddler** | **Birth to 2 Kit**

The Nins Neighborhood is a Montessori-inspired learning tool that enriches sensory perception and cognitive development. Nin figures come in diverse shapes, sizes, and colors, inspiring exploration and skill-building activities like sorting, matching, and categorizing. These activities enhance visual perception, fine motor skills, and hand-eye coordination while fostering creativity and language development through imaginative play.

Each of the Nins Neighborhood pieces originates from a family-owned business that was born from the desire for open-ended play for their own children. Their wooden toys are crafted from sustainably sourced wood; meticulously hand-painted with water-based, child-safe dye; and finished with a coating of natural wax and vegetable-based oil. From design to production, each piece is created with care in Spain, ensuring quality and safety for your little ones. Piece colors will vary.

Scheduling

We suggest getting the Nins Neighborhood out at least twice a week and enjoying it with your child. There are many educational activities that you can do with the Nins Neighborhood. You can focus on one at a time or combine as many as you like!

1. Fine Motor Skills
The Nin figures and their accessories are an excellent way to develop your toddler's fine motor skills. Placing the Nins into the barrels and rings works on the pincer grasp that builds muscles for eventual writing skills.

You can begin by encouraging your child to remove the Nins from the rings. Next, your child can place the Nins in the rings or containers. You can start with just a few or let your child have fun with all of them. Hand-over-hand assistance often helps this click for your child.

2. Sorting and Mathematics
Parents can use Nin characters as hands-on manipulatives to teach a range of mathematical concepts, including counting, sorting, colors, correspondence, and sequencing.

Counting: Have your child count with you as you put figures into a story.

Sorting: Ask your child to help you sort the pieces. Coach him to put coins with coins, rings with rings, etc.

Colors: Have your little one put Nins into a container of the same color or place a matching ring over a Nin. It can be beneficial to start by only setting out a few colors. Then work up to more and more until your child can match all of the figures.

Correspondence: You can also practice one-to-one correspondence by setting out the same number of rings and figures and having your child place one on each.

Older Children: As a bonus, older children can use the Nins Neighborhood pieces to practice more advanced math skills. These include building basic sequences (such as coin, ring, coin, ring) or practical addition and subtraction as Nins join or leave the storyline. These are fun skills to work on as your toddler grows into the pre-K years or to engage older

siblings or friends who will inevitably want to join in your toddler's fun.

3. Storytelling and Problem-Solving
Nins Neighborhood is a uniquely multifaceted resource, but we have listed it in the Emotional Intelligence category for a reason. In our experience using the Nins Neighborhood components, we've found that the story aspect of the pieces powerfully draws in little ones. From the smallest toddlers who are enthralled that the figures can "walk, walk, walk" to preschoolers who participate in complex scenarios, Nins Neighborhood lends itself to social storytelling. Nins Neighborhood can strengthen multiple aspects of verbal skills and emotional intelligence.

Imitation: Your little one will mimic the actions he sees you do as you help the characters move and interact. He will also begin to imitate your words.

Storytelling: The Nin figures enable a tremendous variety of storylines. Your little one will be fascinated as you tell stories of the Nins traveling, playing, building, getting dressed, or going home. The colorful wood containers can be reimagined as train cars, boats, or bathtubs for the Nin characters, and the rings can be hula hoops for jumping or stacked as clothing, life jackets, or towels. The wooden coins serve as stepping stones, fences, or skateboards, offering endless possibilities for creative play. Soon, your little one will add his own opinions on how the story should go and begin to imitate the stories you tell.

Problem-Solving: As you tell stories, you can familiarize your child with resolving social and emotional concerns. "Oh no, Bobby Nin doesn't have a life jacket! Does anyone have one they can share with him?" "Alice Nin is sad because she is lonely. Who could be her friend?" These types of scenarios entrance preschoolers and practice valuable life skills as children help the Nins resolve various situations.

Motor Skills

Let's Get Moving!

From his first grasp of your finger to when those unsteady steps turn into a sprint, your baby's motor skills will improve vastly during these years. From grasping and reaching to vestibular stimulation, the following tools will help set your baby in motion.

Photo: The M. Family in California

Gymnic Physio Roll

Infant | ~~Toddler~~ | Birth to 2 Kit

Unless you've read *Active Baby, Healthy Brain*, the idea of a peanut-shaped exercise ball may seem baffling. But the author explains how an exercise and therapy ball, with its inclination toward instability, will strengthen your baby's core muscles, body awareness, balance, and attention. You can use any exercise ball, but we like the idea of using the Amazing Gymnic Physio Roll. Because of its unique shape, it will roll in only 1 direction, decreasing instability and making it a lot less daunting for new parents to use.

The center of the Gymnic Physio Roll will hold any rider safely within its contoured "saddle," so don't be surprised to find that this Gymnic Physio Roll morphs into a trusty steed for older siblings when baby is napping. If your older child needs a bit of therapy, the Physio Roll is an ideal resource for balance, strengthening, and proprioceptive activities. In fact, the Gymnic brand is one of the most popular brands used by therapists. With a grooved surface for better grip, Physio Roll will hold up to 270 pounds and has a tested load capacity of 660 pounds!

Hand-eye and brain coordination are greatly enhanced by vestibular stimulation, so start early and encourage his developing brain.

Scheduling

0-6 Months
Vestibular stimulation is so important, and rocking your baby gently on the Gymnic Physio Roll is a great way to help him learn to organize the sensory input he receives all day long. Try deflating the ball some for the very young baby and **always** keep safety first.

6-12 Months
As your baby gets stronger, gently increase the intensity of his "workout" to keep it at a level that is fun and interesting. Never get wild with him, though; his brain is fragile, and you don't want to scare him.

12 Months and Up
Vestibular stimulation is just as important as ever, so make sure you work it in every day. Try moving to the rhythm of your favorite music or making up a song to go along with your actions. As always, keep safety first!

Baby Gym Set

Infant | ~~Toddler~~ | Birth to 2 Kit

Research has shown that rhyme awareness positively supports a baby's language development, early literacy, and reading skills. Nursery rhymes provide bite-sized learning opportunities and enable children to recall and memorize word patterns easily.

With their patterns of sounds, rhyming words give a child's developing brain the input it needs to sort words by their sound. This differentiation between syllables and identifying similarities between words that rhyme or begin with the same sounds is a precursor for children to identify the sounds of written words.

Nursery rhymes encourage children to repeat complex groups of sounds to improve their speech with the correct pronunciation.

Both our Baby Gym Set and our Pat-A-Cake books have familiar rhymes and ideas on incorporating the words into gentle play with your baby.

Scheduling

We like to put these books into the daily reading rotation so that they never get overlooked!

Gymnic Over Ball

~~Infant~~ | Toddler | Birth to 2 Kit

Rolling, throwing, catching, and kicking are all skills that improve your little one's coordination and dexterity. One of the best child-friendly balls for that is an Italian import, the Gymnic Over Ball. With its squishy, grippy, lightly textured, and very huggable surface, the Gymnic Over Ball makes catching and throwing super easy.

Children love that it is easy to grasp, while parents appreciate that the Gymnic Over Ball is always light and gentle, making it ideal for indoor play. Even when thrown at full strength, the soft Gymnic Over Ball will barely sting. It's easy to inflate by mouth, so you can fold it and take it with you. It is safe for all ages, but parental supervision is recommended to ensure your child doesn't try to chew the ball or play with the air plug.

Scheduling

Babies
Gymnic Over Ball integrates well into some *Active Baby, Healthy Brain* activities. During playtime, older babies who are crawling and sitting can learn to easily roll the Gymnic Ball and catch it when it is rolled to them.

Young Toddlers
The size of the Gymnic Over Ball makes it a bit cumbersome for young babies to catch, but for toddlers, it shines. Gymnic Over Ball's larger size makes it a superb tool to teach young toddlers rudimentary catching and kicking skills.

Older Toddlers
If you're looking for fun active games for older toddlers, Gymnic Over Ball lends itself well to basketball (with a box or wastepaper can on a chair), bowling (with empty or slightly filled water bottles), soccer (with a box tipped on its side), and innumerable other toddler sports. Besides expending energy, these activities help develop hand-eye coordination, motor planning, reflexes, and (depending on what you play) the important life skills of sportsmanship and taking turns.

Pat-a-Cake

~~Infant~~ | Toddler | Birth to 2 Kit

Nursery rhymes offer all the benefits of rhythm and predictability, along with an often-captivating storyline.

Did you know that rhythm is a huge key to regulation? This is part of why rocking, swinging, or even patting your baby will help him (and you!) calm down. Now you can add reading to the list of rhythms that soothe!

In our home we have found it true that an overtired or otherwise teary child sometimes responds better to the familiar words and actions of a nursery rhyme as both an assistance toward regulation and a pleasant distraction from the sadness of the moment.

Scheduling

With so many fun nursery rhymes included, we suggest reading 1 or 2 a day.

Sensory Skills

What's So Important about the Sensory System?

The ability to interpret your senses and feel what you're feeling is remarkable! Babies are wired to notice textures and colors, wrestle gravity with increasing confidence, and gain increasingly precise control of their muscles. These are all sensory skills.

Many books have been written on sensory processing, and it is well worth the time to understand this subject deeply. But for today, let's just talk about proprioception, or the ability to understand where your body is in space. If you cannot sense whether your hand is off the ground, it is going to be pretty tricky to learn to crawl! So any activity that helps your baby observe where his body is (whether that's the Playsilk below or the Gymnic Physio Roll described above in Motor Skills) will help his long-term coordination, stability, and ease in everyday life.

Using positive sensory stimulation (through all the senses) in brief intervals will help these sensory pathways to become strong and therefore achieve a sense of permanent learning.

Researchers believe that beginning at about 3 months, babies need intentional sensory stimulation to nurture intellectual growth. They claim that if we address it early enough, we can prevent the all-encompassing and debilitating functional impact that sensory processing disorders can have on a child.

There are countless ways to do this, and these tools are just a start. Make sure to integrate as many sensory experiences into daily life as is possible—from stroking velvet to digging through rice and squashing mud pies.

We've seen a lot of sensory challenges in our house (Occupational therapy is so helpful!), but we've also seen some huge wins. When your toddler tornado can actually sit down to work on a puzzle, your child who can't stand textures allows some ice cream on his face, or your baby finally enjoys playing in the grass this summer, you'll find that all the hard work is paying off!

Peek & Pull Baby Tissue Box

Infant | ~~Toddler~~ | **Birth to 2 Kit**

Babies love unpacking tissue boxes, so Sensory Sprouts developed a safe and fun alternative, the Peek & Pull Baby Tissue Box. The Peek & Pull begins with a soft yet durable oversized tissue box. Inside, your baby will discover 7 scarves, each featuring a different texture for tactile exploration. He will practice his pincer grip as he grabs the scarves and learn about object permanence as he reaches into the box for more items to pull out.

This box was created to address multiple sensory needs, and you can add items from around the home to provide a stimulating environment as your baby explores the world around him. This exclusive set also includes a super-soft minky crinkle cloth for baby's sensory exploration.

Why not add a fun twist and hide objects in the tissues for him to discover? It'll be a great challenge for your baby's sorting skills. And with the sweet home theme, toddlers will love putting other toys in and out as they play.

Older siblings (or your baby as he grows) will find the tissues ideal for pretend play as he changes his baby doll or wipes his teddy bear's nose.

Scheduling

Introduce this to baby as soon as he seems interested—probably around 6 months old. Younger babies will likely enjoy crinkling and examining the "tissues", then pulling them out of the box, then putting them in and out for play.

Playsilk

Infant | ~~Toddler~~ | Birth to 2 Kit

Simple and natural, Playsilks have been recommended for nearly 100 years to encourage children to use their imagination and creativity. The sumptuously soft feel of Playsilks is ideal for developing babies. Wispy enough for a tiny baby to manipulate, Playsilks provide a wonderful sensory experience. They are great for peek-a-boo, and the lovely texture and translucency of the Playsilk makes it ideal for hiding-and-finding games with your baby. Easily stuffed into a diaper bag or purse, Playsilks make a soft, easy-to-pack "comfy" for traveling little ones.

As your babies grow, so does the versatility of their Playsilk. Watch them become princes and princesses or put on a cape and practice dragon-slaying. Wrap a baby doll, hoist a flag, or set the table for a tea party; there are unlimited hours of open-ended play with a Playsilk.

Silk is remarkably durable and can withstand years of play. We recommend hand washing with warm water and a mild soap, then drying in a dryer set on low for a few minutes to restore the softness and remove wrinkles. For some reason, many children enjoy washing their Playsilks and hanging them outside to dry. It is a wonderfully peaceful experience, so let them do this often!

Scheduling

Unlimited!

Chomp and Chew Hexagonal Teether and Lil' Dimpl

Infant | ~~Toddler~~ | Birth to 2 Kit

With 2 levels of softness and 6 different textures, the Chomp and Chew Hexagonal Teether is perfect for sore gums.

There are a lot of teethers on the market, but what drew us to the Chomp and Chew is its easy-to-grip handle. Many babies begin to teethe at 3 months but lack the manual dexterity to manage the typical teether. But the Chomp and Chew has both easy-to-grip sides and a flexible strap across the center.

The multiple sensory points and textures offer pain relief to tender gums, helping reduce the baby's fussiness and discomfort. The one-piece construction makes the Chomp and Chew safe and easy to clean.

This teether meets or exceeds ASTM and CPSIA safety regulations and is free of BPA/PVC/phthalates and lead.

Lil Dimpl is a great sensory development tool for babies. Made of soft, safe, food-grade silicone, Lil Dimpl is a flexible friend for your infant to explore with his hands or his mouth.

Lil Dimpl can be stretched, squished, and gummed and because of its free-flowing open design, it is easy for babies to hang onto.

Babies will love poking and popping Lil Dimpl's noggin when they get a bit older. Dishwasher safe. Available in assorted colors.

Scheduling

Unlimited! Use both as desired for teething, playtime, car trips, or any other time it suits you and your baby.

Zippee

Infant | ~~Toddler~~ | Birth to 2 Kit

Babies seem universally attracted to long, thin, often dangerous objects. The Zippee activity toy provides a fun, safe, and educational substitute for your charging cable, sneaker shoelaces, or drapery cord.

Designed in collaboration with doctors and therapists, Zippee's flexible and soft edges, textured cords, and comfortable-to-hold grips create a clean, safe, and therapeutic alternative.

Babies and toddlers will love pulling Zippee's cables from one side of the pod to the other as they marvel over their cleverness. Plus, many Zippee textured cords produce a muted sound and intriguing vibration when pulled through the capsule.

Zippee is made from food-grade silicone and is BPA-free and phthalate-free.

Scheduling

Unlimited!

Articles

From Our Family to Yours

39 Years of Serving You

In 1985, we were a family of 5. I was the oldest of 3 toddler girls with a mom who absolutely excelled at educating us at home. This was during the "Dark Ages" of homeschooling, and online searching was still a thing of the future. Our mom, Deb, was (and is) a voracious reader and an avid researcher. We girls were thriving academically, and other moms were naturally interested in using the same curricula Deb had found.

That same year, she and Dan, our dad, repurposed the business license originally intended for their world-class Golden Retriever breeding operation, which had come to naught, and she launched Timberdoodle, a homeschool supply company. She created our first catalog, and growth came fast. We shipped curriculum from our laundry room, our grandparents' basement, and finally warehouses and an office. Two more children were added to the family, and we all grew up working in the business from an early age.

Now, decades later, Timberdoodle is still renowned for out-of-the-box learning and crazy-smart finds. Mom's engineering background has heavily influenced our STEM selections and warehouse layout, and her no-nonsense, independent approach has made these kits the award-winning choice that they are today.

All 5 of us children are grown now, and most still work at Timberdoodle in key roles. Our brother and his wife have welcomed 4 amazing little ones in the past 7 years, and we sisters have opened our home to children through foster care and adoption. As our families have grown, we've become even more committed to equipping parents with the best homeschooling resources. The kits we sell are the same ones we use in our own homes, and we hope you enjoy them as much as we do.

In the following articles, you'll hear Deb and others talk about some of the nitty-gritty questions we receive. Do you have a question not answered here? You are invited to contact us at any time—we'd love to help!

Joy (for all of us)

Picture circa 1989, breaking ground for our first warehouse!

Homeschooling Your Baby: Learning Styles

Originally Written in 1993, Shortly after the Addition of Pearl, Baby #5.

Having a newborn has reminded us again of why we teach our children at home. Teaching your child does not begin with kindergarten curriculum, nor does it begin with a preschool program or even with your baby's first step. Home education begins shortly after birth; it begins with a cuddle.

Doesn't it seem that after you have your baby, everyone rushes to hold her? Our baby Pearl is no exception. She loves all the attention and seems to adore everyone who dotes on her. However, do not put her on your shoulder to cuddle. She will arch her back and let you know clearly that this is NOT where she belongs. Is she being difficult, acting spoiled, showing her sin nature already? If we had assumed that, then we would have missed a wonderful opportunity to nurture our baby.

Instead, we recognized that Pearl is a visual baby, which means that she is wired to learn best by seeing the world around her. When people put Pearl on their shoulder, it limits her field of vision and thwarts her primary objective of seeing everything. In other words, they are incapacitating her learning agenda. But by holding her against themselves, face forward, she gets to see all that they see, and she is not only content but is still able to fulfill her consuming passion to learn. Babies are born learning machines, and learning is their first priority. But not all babies are visual babies.

Abel, our son, was an auditory baby, which means he learned best by hearing and experimenting with sound. As a baby, he loved to be cuddled on our shoulders, as close to our voice-box as possible. To soothe him we would merely hum, and he would be so fascinated with the sound that he would soon forget his discomfort.

Auditory babies are frustrated by a lot of noise because they want to sort out each sound, and the combination of sounds is overwhelming. When things are dull, auditory babies can create their own excitement with various chirps, coos, and patter. Even at this tender age they delight in listening to themselves "speak." Get used to the sound of their voice because you are going to hear a lot of it!

A third type of baby scholar is the hands-on learner. Whereas the auditory or visual learner can satisfy his enthusiasm for investigating by sitting in your arms, the hands-on learner needs to be doing. Our daughter Hope was this type of learner. She would wiggle and squirm and move about just for the sheer pleasure it brought her. The saying "motion stops commotion" particularly suits this style of learner. She did not want to sit quietly, and had she been forced to, it would not have been in her best interest.

Bear in mind that we are not addressing areas of discipline here. There will undoubtedly be times when your wiggler needs to sit still for a medical exam, your auditory baby will need to be quiet during a meeting, and your visual baby may need to duck under a blanket to be nursed.

However, for the nurturing parent, these times should be the exception and not the norm. The wiggler should not only be allowed to move about freely; she should be encouraged to do so. Again, thwarting this drive will impede the learning process.

The first step to teaching your baby at home is to let your baby teach you. What makes your baby laugh? All sorts of tickles will amuse your wiggler but leave your auditory baby sober. However, he will squeal with delight whenever Grandpa makes a funny sound. Your visual baby will love contorted faces and other forms of slapstick humor.

By doing your "homework" and studying your infant, you will often discover what sort of learner he is. By determining what will soothe your baby and what amuses him, you will not only have one of your biggest clues as to what style of learner he is, but you will also be well on your way to nurturing a lifelong love of learning.

Homeschooling Your Baby: The Ideal Environment

Originally Written in 1993, Shortly after the Addition of Pearl, Baby #5.

As a teaching mom, my first assignment is to study my baby and learn how she learns best. Keep in mind that many babies are a blend of styles, but all babies will have a decided preference.

When you are the parent of a visual baby, the road ahead of you will be fairly smooth. For whatever reason, nearly all canned curriculum is geared to the visual learner. Moreover, visual children who attend school have the greatest opportunity for success because most of their teachers will not only use a visual curriculum but are also visual learners themselves.

Visual babies study the details in the world around them. These are the babies who become the children that seem to teach themselves to read. Our daughter Joy was reading words at 18 months and loving it! Because we know Pearl is likewise a visual baby, we will work to surround her with lots of visual stimulation. The easiest way for me to do this is through brightly colored picture books, but other ideas are posters, mirrors, toys, even a fish tank! My goal is to nourish the visual ability of my baby and to allow her to excel in an area in which she is very capable.

Our auditory babies have also picked up academic skills readily. The advantage they have is that nearly all my teaching is given orally first. This has given them at least one opportunity to master what is expected, and because auditory learners are so experienced at processing what they hear, they tend to be very successful.

We have found that our auditory babies are ideal candidates for music training and foreign languages. An environment with good music will begin a lifetime love of music. If we were bilingual, we would have capitalized on that skill while they were still infants. Instead, we did the next best thing and let them listen in while we played foreign language tapes.

A lesson we learned the hard way was to spend as much time as possible talking to our babies while there was still time. Before we knew it, they were talking, talking, talking. And that will continue throughout their childhood as they sing while they work, chant out their math facts, and yodel for the sheer pleasure of it. If it seems to you that their mouths are always in gear, keep in mind they truly do need to hear themselves think.

In the academic world, our hands-on babies are at a disadvantage. These children learn best by doing, but apart from some preschool/kindergarten activities, most curriculum is geared for visual learners. Our Hope needed an environment full of action. Hope was not content to sit and watch the action flow around her. As soon as possible, she hurled herself into that action.

Hands-on babies learn by feeling and doing, so give them every opportunity to push, pull, squeeze, squish, dig, and dump. When Hope was a little older and involved in "hard-core academics" like puzzles and coloring, it amused us to no end to notice that she spent the entire morning standing at her child-size table.

To ask her to sit down to work on a puzzle would have bewildered her. How can you possibly do a puzzle without hopping, wiggling, or at the very least marching in place?! We could have forced her to sit quietly in a chair for schoolwork, but she would have been so engrossed in the labor of sitting still that there would have been no brain power left to solve puzzles. We saved the training of sitting still for when sitting still was the only goal.

Keep in mind that those wiggles are wired into your baby. When you think you just cannot clean up one more mess, tell yourself that to excel academically, your baby needs as much active time as possible. I like to think that the wearier I am, the brighter my hands-on baby is becoming.

Once more, we are not addressing conduct here. We do not think we should abdicate our throne to a 15-pound tyrant. We do, however, have the intent of making our baby a course of intense study. What makes him sad and what makes him happy? What challenges him and what does he find boring? The more I know about my baby, the easier and more pleasant my career as a teaching parent will be.

Get Into a Routine You Love

Babies Are Unpredictable—Or Are They?

Humans seem to thrive on routine. Perhaps you start your day with coffee or take time each evening to read. We like to get outside every morning and eat fun foods on Sunday. Your littlest human is no different!

Babies and toddlers are stuck in a world they cannot control, and they do not have the communication skills to even express their desires. A simple way to help them is to start early with routines.

Tiny Routines

A newborn's life introduces his first routines. "I cry = they come" is the foundation of connection and so important right now. Little things help too. Perhaps you always use Play Together Caterpillar right after you change his diaper or do a bedtime routine of bath and lotion before swaddling him for bed. If he can predict what will happen next, his life becomes ordered rather than chaotic.

Routines Together

As he gets older, routines will seem more helpful for you than him. For instance, if you know that your reading time is maximized just after his nap or that your best window for getting outside is midmorning, your day has a framework to it.

Our family finds that it usually takes a while to settle into a comfortable routine when a new little one joins our family. During the in-between time, stress levels are higher, and we spend more time trying to figure out what to do next than we do actually getting stuff done.

Once we have a framework in place, everyone relaxes. We know that the morning nap happens at 10:00 and that this will be our best chance to work at the table with the big kids.

We also know that there is a block of time in the afternoon that we can do pretty much anything with, and we have a running list of things to slide into that spot. If it's rainy or super hot, I might reach for the watercolors and library books. If it's a lovely day, let's get outside to ride bikes or play with the hose. Should we succumb to a cold or find everyone is a bit on the grumpy side for another reason, we might do Mad Mattr and audiobooks.

How to Begin

Grab pen and paper and take a moment to think through things you already do. This can be as simple as the morning nap or as complex as the every-other-week playgroup. Now make a list of the things you'd like to add. Perhaps you don't have an established reading time yet, or you feel like a dedicated walking time would benefit the whole family.

Block Planning

Every family is different, so take this next part with a particular grain of salt, but our family loves planning in blocks and routines rather than in minutes. It is a lot less pressure to know that the littles will do their list after breakfast but before our walk instead of thinking it must happen between 7:15 and 8:10.

Put It on Paper

Find a way to make your new schedule usable for you. Perhaps it's as simple as a sticky note at the changing table reminding you to do a sensory activity. Or perhaps you love a color-coded chart with hourly instructions. Do what works best for you!

Don't forget that your schedule customizer can be the backbone of your planning. You can use it for a weekly checklist or a daily plan—whatever works best for you.

Contingency Planning

I find that I'm a much more peaceful parent if I have several contingencies up my sleeve. These can be as simple as the playdough set or a coloring book and favorite music. Knowing that if I have an unanticipated block of time I could do X or Y makes life so much less stressful. I usually write a few ideas down at the beginning of a new season, and soon I'm able to improvise without that prop. (And, of course, if the children all spontaneously play beautifully together, I'm not going to interrupt that, but knowing that a little structure goes a long way for some of our crew, I'm better off being prepared!)

Wall Charts

We started doing visual routines for a few of our older children and were shocked when our then 13-month-old loved it most of all. We did a traditional pocket chart just out of reach and would ask her "Did you brush your teeth?" to which she'd either bob excitedly up and down nodding or dash to the bathroom with a grin to get that done. So we'd suggest trying it with even a young toddler and seeing how it works for you.

Settle In and Change It Up

As your little ones grow, you'll constantly be tweaking the schedule—fewer naps, longer times between feedings, more interest in activities, the seasonal shifts of the weather, etc. When you notice something is no longer working well for you, just tweak that block of time and you'll be good to go again!

Our Family's Routine

The Thrill of Controlled Chaos

Our daily routine shifts often, but since it can be inspirational to see what other families are doing, here is our routine in 2 versions roughly 2 years apart.

2020

This first schedule is from spring of 2020, when our little ones consisted of a 2-year-old and twin 4-year-olds:

4:00-5:00 AM: Our youngest gets up without fail and often reads, plays quietly, or does playdough at the table. If we're feeling particularly motivated, we use that one-on-one time to work on his "school work," which he absolutely loves.

6:00 AM: The other kids get up and have some time to either read or color until they are ready for breakfast. They are also free to start on their morning list if they are eager to get done and start playing.

The next block is breakfast. Usually this happens at 6:30 or 7:00, but there is flexibility for mornings when people wake up hungry or with a burning desire to draw something before breakfast.

After breakfast everyone does his list. Right now each child has a few simple things to do, like getting dressed, brushing teeth, fixing his bed, and some age-appropriate household chores. Those who finish fast will get to play until the next thing starts.

Somewhere around 8:00 AM, Grandma jumps in to teach school with Pearl. Everyone looks forward to this special time! She works off the children's lists and adds in books and things they enjoy. This lasts anywhere from 30 to 60 minutes.

The next block of time is typically a walk outside, but if weather or sickness precludes that, then it is a great time for more active play indoors.

By mid-morning our youngest has hit his limit and heads to a nap. Now is the perfect time for more focused academics for the older crew, intricate art projects, or chapter books. This tends to be a big block of time and is sometimes broken up by free play. "Go play for 5 minutes, then come back and do your next page."

Lunch is next and may be eaten at the table or outside on the playground or as a picnic while watching the construction on the new warehouse.

Afterwards we are usually eager to get outside again. The big kids have a quiet time somewhere in here too. The length of that varies with how much rest is needed and how long the little guy's nap went, etc.

At 2:00 it is time for a change. If we've been playing outside, it's probably time to come in and calm down indoors for a bit. If we've been inside, it's an optimal time to get out and play or walk down to say hi to Great-Grandma. In the summer this is our swimming time. On the wet days of winter it's a perfect time to bundle up for a short walk, then do STEM or art indoors.

Finally, our family steps into the dinner and evening routine, which often includes reading library books before jammies, devotions, and more books before bed.

Not every day is like this. Wednesday is OT day, so all must shift to accommodate driving to and from the appointment.

Sickness, doctor appointments, new babies, and even handling an influx of orders at work will rock the schedule. However, having a framework in place gives us the flexibility to shift some things without having the whole day collapse into a muddle.

2022

This second schedule is from spring of 2022, when our crew of 5 kids now included a 1-year-old, 2-year-old, 3-year-old, and twin 6-year-olds!

6:00 AM: Everyone gets up, (baby usually rises by 5AM) and most of the crew moves right into breakfast. This is one of my favorite read-aloud times on a calm morning. A fresh library book can do wonders for the mood!

After breakfast everyone does their morning list. Those who finish fast will get to play until 8:00.

At about 8:00 AM we move into table work. (This one has a set time so as to reward the diligent workers with a predictable amount of playtime.) School time with five littles is often chaotic, and never boring! The toddler is thrilled to be able to put together single-piece puzzles, so I often start with that. Eventually she gets down and plays with her "school time" toys like Once Upon a STEM, puzzles and shapesorters, and even Playmobil.

The 2-year-old does her preschool work in short spurts. A page of work, a puzzle, a little cutting, etc.

The 3-year-old is doing end-of-preschool work, along with All About Reading Prereading. All 3 littles usually tag along for sweet Ziggy!

The twins are finishing kindergarten right now, and often will work on smart games, handwriting, art, or other assignments that don't need much handholding.

The preschoolers will usually work on either side of me so that I'm able to start one, then help the other, then jump back to redirect the first one.

Grandma and Pearl are doing special school time during this morning block too—a treat for everyone!

The next block is typically a walk outside, but if weather or sickness precludes that, then it is a great time for playdough, dress-up, or swinging and playing indoors.

By mid-morning everyone is ready for a recharge, and we typically serve snacks outside if the weather is tolerable. We intentionally leave a good block of time for outdoor play here. We have a large play field with various farm animals, a sandbox, slackline, bikes, ninja line, garden, and more. Reality check though—the kids seem to spend most of their time chasing, digging, or stacking things right now! So there are many treasure holes and piles of logs/bamboo/toys representing whatever airplane/boat/house has captured their imagination!

Naptime is around 11:00/11:30 for our 3 youngest. This becomes the perfect time for more focused academics for the older crew, more intricate art projects, or elaborate LEGO time.

Lunch is next and may be eaten at the table or outside as a picnic in the field.

At 2:00 it is typically time to go outdoors and play/garden/visit Great-Grandma, etc. This is our least structured block of the day and can be modified to fit the day's needs.

Finally, our family steps into the dinner and evening routine, which often includes library books, dinner, clean-up, jammies, devotions, and more books before bed.

9 Tips for Homeschooling with a Toddler

Successfully Integrating Your Toddler into a Busy Homeschool

As your baby becomes a toddler, you'll love his enthusiastic, loving, curious, confident, and innocent nature. However, to a home-educating mom, he will also be exhausting, impatient, loud, and unpredictable. So how can we incorporate him with the older children in our education program without overwhelming anyone? Here are some ideas that have worked for us.

1. Keep It Fun

Your goal is productive learning, and that can be accomplished through many fun methods. If your child is not easily making the transition to being required to accomplish something, don't hesitate to bring out some motivators.

Why not make a chore board of all the different tasks you would like to accomplish in a week with your child, then let him choose which one he would like to do next. Photos work great as cheap and easy chore cards. Flip over the finished task card, and you will move through all your goals for your child while also engaging him in the process. Even at this young age, you can begin to teach him how to structure his day independently.

Or let your toddler earn a reward for finishing the tasks. For instance, have him pick out six tasks to do (using the picture cards again), and when the tasks are finished, he has earned the privilege of playing outside, listening to his music, or whatever else you find that is motivating to him.

Our household currently uses a letterboard listing each child's name and felt stars. As a child completes something off his list, we add a star to the board. When he has 5 stars, he is done for now and free to play with the "reward" item of his choice. Right now sensory bins and a box of little cars are big hits with our preschoolers, while the bigger kids want to earn LEGO® time or a break in the schedule to create elaborate paper contraptions.

2. Keep It Short

Keep the structured projects short and varied. Your toddler is much more likely to stay engaged for an hour if he has 6 to 10 short projects rather than spending all that time tracing letters. You can set him up for longer periods of time with activities he already enjoys such as water play, coloring, and more; but for structured learning, begin small.

3. Add a Story

Our boys enjoy Can You Find Me? riddles a lot more when they are "catching the bad guy" than if they are just asked to solve a puzzle. Our little girls find tracing a lot more fun if they are helping the animals get home rather than matching them.

When one child had difficulty tracing, we even brought out fish crackers and set up a story where the fish needed to get home. As the child traced the line, the fish followed, and when she reached the end of each line she got to eat the fish.

4. Use All Your Child's Senses

Don't get tunnel vision by focusing only on workbook-type tasks; there will be plenty of years for that later. Work to incorporate all your child's senses as you do different activities. The weekly checklist will help you be aware of what activities you've already done each week so that you don't accidentally overlook anything.

5. Keep It Flexible

For a toddler, living is learning. New things, experiences, and skills to be learned surround your child. Structure is good, but don't forget that you can relax and enjoy the moment. If you don't get to puzzles this week, don't sweat it! If your toddler loves to paint, take time to encourage more painting. All of life is learning, so have fun and relax!!

6. Incorporate Them When You Can

Most toddlers will be blissful if you let them participate in your art lessons. If you are using expensive supplies that they will destroy, try buying inexpensive sets that are just for them.

It helps to buy an art bin or caddy to store all their supplies in (markers, glue sticks, scissors, stickers, and so forth). Not only will this encourage orderliness, but toddlers love to sift and sort through their possessions.

7. Just for School Time

Our most obvious suggestion: keep a box or a shelf of items that can only be used during the "big kids" school time. This can include items from this kit and/or other art supplies, workbooks, puzzles, blocks, and hands-on materials that are brought out only during this time. This distinction will add to their attractiveness and make the "learning hour" something your preschooler will anticipate every day!

8. Scaffold His Learning

It is as great a temptation to over-coach your child as it is to expect too much. You'll want to evaluate how much he is capable of today and encourage him to reach that full potential. Showing him exactly what to do doesn't give him time to understand and process his options himself. Don't steal his "Aha!" moments! At the same time, frustrating a child by expecting him to correctly understand every concept the first time won't help either. No parent perfectly scaffolds his or her child's learning, but being aware of the hazards of both extremes is a wonderful start.

9. Work Yourself Out of a Job

Helping your child learn is a thrill you'll likely never outgrow, but that doesn't mean you have to hold his hand for each puzzle piece. Be deliberate about having him put in the last piece completely by himself, then the last two, and so on, until he finds he can do the whole thing by himself.

If you have a child who prefers to work only hand-in-hand with you, it may work best to plan ahead and set up situations where doing it himself becomes most desirable. For instance, your toddler wants down from his high chair, and you want that last puzzle piece placed. You could hover or you could help, but what if instead you were suddenly very busy in the kitchen. "I can help you in a few minutes. Or if you get it in yourself, I can stop and get you down." No, it's not rocket science, but it does help encourage those little hands to try once more!

Can We Talk about Obedience?

Why Work on Following Directions with a Toddler?

Have you ever felt that teaching a toddler to obey feels like a lot of work and conflict for little reward? It is work—a ton of work, but let us just encourage you that it is time well spent.

We don't want to crush your toddler's spirit or inspire you to play the role of total dictator, but a child who can follow directions will have a lot more fun and freedom in his life! If it is any comfort, I'm typing these words moments after working with our resident toddler on not pulling hair for approximately the millionth time…so I totally get the exhaustion of this goal!

Not sure where to start? Keep it really simple. Our top 3 priorities are:

- come
- no/don't touch
- kind hands

We find that usually covers the biggest issues, from power cords to baby brother's hair, without multiplying expectations for a little one.

Come—The Gift That Keeps Giving

The "come" direction is possibly the biggest safety issue and also works really well for teaching anything else. For instance, if he's discovered some new way to annoy his siblings across the room while you're feeding the newborn (and it's always while you're feeding the newborn), how amazing would it be to tell him to come and have him obey?

We have a few practical tips for you:

1. Keep Commands to a Minimum
Again, you want to avoid the role of dictator in your child's life. You are his boss, his coach, his protector, and so much more, but sometimes in our eagerness to help him stay on the right track we get carried away with micromanaging.

2. All Commands Must Be Obeyed
If he only needs to come when you have your hands free, he hasn't really learned to obey. Yes, it's exhausting, but if you want to help him learn obedience, you need to be consistent in your expectations.

3. Give Grace and Assistance
Simple hand-over-hand coaching after saying "Come!", followed by copious amounts of praise, will remedy so many incidents of disobedience with a toddler. We're not talking about acting a drill sergeant and angrily putting your child in time-out every time he doesn't come fast enough, but we are looking to teach him HOW to do what you expect.

4. Keep Your Words Few
For a nearly verbal child, it is not going to work well for you to say "Come" sometimes, and other times say "Get over here, please," and still other times "It's almost time to get going. I need to grab your coat and hat. Come here, honey, we are going to…oh, wait, there's the coat. Anyway, get over here so I can help with your shoes." The more you talk with baby the better, but particularly when teaching a new command, keep your wording precise and clear: "Franklin, come!"

5. Make a Plan

What's important to you in training your child? Our family values staying connected, feeling safe, being gentle and kind, staying calm and consistent, and giving clear explanations.

A program some of us have used and greatly respect, Connected Families, phrases their perspective as a foundation of safety, followed by love/connection, then coaching our called and capable children, and finally correcting since they are responsible for their actions. If your expectations of yourself as a parent/teacher are clear, then you'll be better able to implement them in the chaos of daily life.

How Does Homeschooling Help with Obedience?

At this age, "school work" is an invaluable training ground for obedience. You have the advantage of structure and natural opportunities to cheer your child on as he does what you've asked. You also have the ability to gently help him obey with your hand over his if he just doesn't want to this morning.

You absolutely need to be sensitive to the child who had a rough night teething or the little one who is completely overwhelmed by the loud fireworks outside. At the same time, puzzles and other formal learning moments are the perfect opportunity to practice obeying. Fun and friendly practice will build your child's ability to persevere, and we bet you'll be surprised when he gets to the point that he actually looks forward to doing activities he has sometimes refused in the past.

10 Reasons to Stop Schoolwork and Go Build Something!

Photo: The M. Family in California

Would you like to supplement your curriculum with a program that simultaneously improves your child's visual and spatial perception, fine motor skills, patience, problem-solving, creativity, ability to follow directions, prereading skills, grasp of physics concepts, and engineering ability? Better yet, what if your child would actually enjoy this curriculum and choose to do it whenever he could? No, this isn't some mythical homeschool product guaranteed to solve all your problems. We are talking about the Lego bricks already strewn throughout your house, the ThinkPlay blocks in our preschool curriculum, and the Bioloid robot kit designed for teens.

Construction kits just might be the most underrated type of curriculum ever. It's not just us; research concludes that children learn a lot by designing and building things. Would you agree that construction is one of the most valuable educational processes available? Here are 10 skills your child will learn with his construction kit.

1. Visual Perception

It may be obvious that it takes visual perception to find the right pieces and place them where they belong, but consider that whether your child is reading, finishing a puzzle, or doing open-heart surgery, proficiency in visual perception is mandatory.

2. Fine Motor Skills

Boys especially seem to struggle with fine motor skills, particularly when it comes to writing and drawing. Amazingly enough, though, they are often the most passionate about building—the natural remedy! The more they fine-tune their dexterity, the easier school time becomes for both of you.

3. Patience

Do you know anyone who couldn't use more patience? Construction takes time. Slowing down, reading directions, starting over when you make a mistake or a sibling knocks over your creation…these are all valuable character-building experiences.

4. Problem-Solving

Some children lack the ability to troubleshoot a situation and figure out the next step. Construction sets provide a structured opportunity to figure out what went wrong and to fix it if you are following the directions. If you are designing your own models, you'll have even more opportunities to solve problems.

5. Spatial Perception

Probably the clearest picture of how important it is to be able to mentally convert 2D images into 3 dimensions is that of a surgeon. Knowing where the spleen is on a 2D textbook page isn't nearly the same thing as being able to reach into an incision and find the damaged organ.

6. Creativity

Not every creative person has artistic ability. But construction can open the doors of creativity like no other tool. What if I move this gear over here? Could I build that bridge with only blue pieces?

7. Following Directions

Some children are natural rule followers and need to be encouraged to be creative. Others need constraint to follow directions, at least on occasion. If your child falls into that camp, construction kits are a natural way to encourage him in this skill, with the added benefit of a finished result he can show off.

8. Prereading Skills

Did you know that a child who cannot duplicate a pattern will be a poor candidate for reading and writing? Not only that, but the use of pattern duplication is a proven way to help prepare children to understand abstract math concepts and higher-order thinking. But if you have a scholar who rolls his eyes at working with pattern blocks and sighs deeply when asked to replicate a design with traditional 4-sided blocks, you need construction kits.

9. Grasp of Physics

Friction, force, mass, and energy are concepts of basic physics—each much more easily explained and grasped with a set of blocks and a ball than by studying a dry textbook definition.

10. Engineering Ability

Many "born engineers" are not drawn to textbooks. But set a construction kit in front of them and watch them explore pulleys, levers, wheels, and gears. They'll soon go from exploration to innovation, and you'll be amazed at their inventions.

9 Tips for Homeschooling Gifted Children

From a Family Who Knows This Journey

1. Disdain Busywork

Your child wants to learn, so don't slow him down! If he has mastered multiplication, why are you still spending an hour a day reviewing it? Yes, he does need some review, but we've seen way too many families focus on completing every problem rather than mastering the material. One way to test this is to have him complete every other review problem on only the most essential pages and see how he does. If he can prove he knows it, he doesn't need to be spending quite as much time there.

2. Go Deep

Allow breathing room in your schedule so you have time to investigate earth's gravitational pull or the advantages and disadvantages of hair sheep vs. woolly sheep. Remember that your child is asking to learn, so why pull him away from the subject that's fascinating him? After all, we know that material we're interested in sticks with us so much better than things we learn only because we must.

3. Go Fast

If your child wants to take 3 science courses this year or race through 2 math levels, then why not let him? Homeschoolers can absolutely rock this because there is no one holding us to a "traditional" pace!

4. Encourage Completion

Sometimes it seems there is a touch of ADD in every genius. Give your child as much flexibility as you possibly can, but also keep in mind that you'll be doing him a disservice if he never has to complete something he doesn't feel like working on. Sometimes he may even be surprised to realize that the very subject he dreaded is the springboard for a whole new area of investigation!

5. Give Space and Opportunities

If you can keep mandatory studies to a minimum, you'll give your child more opportunities to accelerate his learning in the areas where he is gifted. Common sense, perhaps, but also worth deliberately thinking through as you plan your school year.

6. Work on Weak Areas Carefully

While you definitely want to help your student overcome his struggles, you also want to be careful that a weakness in one area doesn't impede his progress in other ways. For instance, a child may struggle with writing because his brain works much faster than his hands. While we still encourage working on handwriting skills, we also suggest that his parents try teaching him to type and allow him to complete writing assignments on the computer. This lets him continue to build his writing skills instead of holding him back because of his lack of handwriting speed.

7. Emphasize Humility and Service

We have met way too many children who are obnoxiously convinced that they are geniuses and that everyone needs to be in awe of their abilities. Your child will be much healthier (and happier!) if he realizes these 4 things:

- His identity is *never* found in his brainpower.
- Even as gifted as he is, there are still things that others do better than he does.
- Don't weigh him down by constantly telling him how big his brain is. He is much more than his brain. (Should he lose his edge, he won't lose his worth!)
- His gifts are not for himself alone but for serving others.

Of course, the goal is not to shame, insult, or degrade him but to give him a framework from which he can truly thrive and be free to learn. With a proper perspective, he'll be able to enjoy learning without the burden of constantly assessing his genius and worrying what people think of him.

Encourage his learning, but don't forget to cultivate his character. In 10 years, his response to rebuke will be much more telling than his test score this year, so don't put an inordinate amount of stress on intellectual pursuits.

8. Talk—a LOT!

Talk about what he's interested in. Talk about the theories he came up with today. Talk about his daydreams. Talk about what he wants to study next. Talk about why he may actually need to master that most-dreadful-of-subjects, whatever that may be. Not only will you be able to impart your years of wisdom to him, but you'll also know well the subjects he's interested in so you can link those to his other studies, the places you're visiting next week, or that interesting article you read yesterday.

9. Relax!

Your child is a wonderful gift, but don't feel the need to maximize his potential at every moment. As a side benefit, just relaxing about his genius may in fact increase it. Our own family found that some of our best test scores came after a year off of most formal schooling. Not what we would have planned, but a very valuable insight. Living life also equals learning, so maximize that!

Photo: The Siyow Family in Florida

11 Thoughts for Homeschooling Struggling Children

From a Family Who Knows This Journey Too!

If you were to call me up and ask for help with a struggling child, these are some of the questions I might toss your way as our conversation got underway.

What Do You Mean by "Struggling"?

If you tell me that your child stomps his foot and walks away when you mention it's almost school time, I will have a different answer than I will for the child who cries because his math is too complex or the 10-year-old who cannot seem to grasp phonics. Each child is struggling, but the answers must vary! So as you go through my questions here, please disregard any that don't apply and always feel free to reach out to us with a more specific question.

1. Investigate Root Issues

Is every visual task a challenge? Consider a thorough eye and tracking exam. Perhaps phonics are a struggle. How's his hearing? We've had sad, grumpy children respond to addressing underlying health issues like undiagnosed stomach pain, untreated sleep challenges, or vitamin deficiencies. (Don't worry. We aren't about to start preaching certain supplements—but if the idea to consider things like this has never occurred to you, our story may be helpful!) We've also had children whose anxiety or ADHD made it incredibly hard to focus. Knowing *why* something is a struggle may open up new ideas for solving the problem.

2. Embrace Repetition

Does doing more reps solve the problem? If your child finds that a single page of math isn't enough to cement the concept, what if you assign 2 pages? Or if reading is the issue, could you go back to square one with a different program and get a different result?

3. Check His Memory

If you ask him to repeat back random letters or digits, how many can he accurately imitate (e.g., "7, A, Y, 2")? Do this orally to check auditory memory / processing and visually to assess his visual processing / memory.

You generally want to see 7 digits or more in ages 7+. Any less than that and you may have found a huge clue to what skill to work on!

4. Back Up

While you could continue with math work that is on-grade and explain each component over and over, it is highly likely that your student will advance much faster if he starts over with the basics and races through. And he'll do that with less strain on your relationship and less stress for either of you. The same applies to many subjects, particularly if you were not the one who was teaching him when he was at a previous level or if you now know that the old program wasn't using the approach best suited for him.

5. Check Engagement

Is it possible that this is a motivational issue? Even if that is not the primary issue, motivation may help. We have some children who struggle academically due to early life trauma. Rather than throwing up our hands, it has been very helpful to realize that yes, he will work harder at this than his peers might, so he may also need a bigger carrot than his peers. If you pull out all the stops for a week, does that help at all?

6. Really Invest in His Learning Style

How does your child learn best? If he needs auditory repetition, can you record the lesson for him to play back or choose an audio-based course? Or if he's hands-on, make sure you pull out the manipulatives every time for now. Not sure? Take some time to study the skills he has mastered and how he learned them.

7. Make Accommodations

Just as you might do for your gifted child, you want to be careful that a weakness in one area doesn't impede his progress in other ways. For instance, a child may struggle with writing because his brain works much faster than his hands. While we still encourage such a child to work on handwriting skills, we will probably also get him started on typing (TTRS can be very helpful!) and allow him to complete writing assignments on the computer. This lets him continue to build his writing skills instead of holding him back because of his lack of handwriting speed.

For your ADHD child, this may look like installing a trampoline in your dining room and encouraging short breaks to calm his system. What might make this better for him? How do you get there?

8. Timers

We are an ADHD-type household, and one huge impact this has is in time management. Rather than stress over lost time, a visual timer has helped us all. Your student can race the timer, enjoy a special privilege if he beats the timer, or receive practice work if he is opting to daydream instead of working.

9. Emphasize Humility and Service

Just like your gifted child, your struggling child will be much healthier (and happier!) if he realizes these 3 things:
- His identity is *never* found in his brainpower.
- He is indeed gifted in some areas. (Help him find these!)
- His gifts are not for himself alone but for serving others, and he is excellent at that.

Encourage his learning, but don't forget to cultivate his character. In 10 years, his response to rebuke will be much more telling than his test score this year, so don't put an inordinate amount of stress on intellectual pursuits.

10. Tutors

You aren't abdicating your role as a teacher if you realize that separating parenting from math would be helpful for your teen right now!

11. Relax!

When your child is an adult out in the real world, it really won't matter if he learned to read at age 2 or 12. Yes, you want to make progress toward your academic goals, but there is no time limit here!

Living life also equals learning, so engage him in farming, volunteering, swim class, or whatever doors are open, knowing that these are not lesser activities but part of the real work of education. As mentioned elsewhere, our own family found that some of our best test scores came after a year off of most formal schooling. Not what we would have planned, but a very valuable insight.

Convergent & Divergent Thinking
What These Skills Are and Why They Matter

Have you considered the necessity of incorporating both convergent and divergent thinking into your learning time? Experts recognize these as the 2 major types of brain challenges every human encounters.

Does that just sound like a whole bunch of big words? No worries—let's break it down. Your child needs to be able to find the right answer when needed (math, medicine dosage) and also needs to be able to come up with a creative, unscripted answer when the situation warrants (art, architecture).

A child who can only find the "right" answer will be a rigid thinker who can't problem-solve well or think outside the box.

A child who only thinks creatively will not be able to follow procedures or do anything that involves math.

Photo: The Melendez Kids in Honduras

What Is Convergent Thinking?
Convergent thinking generally involves finding a single best answer and is important in the study of math and science. Convergent thinking is the backbone of the majority of curricula and is crucial for future engineers, doctors, and even parents. Much of daily life is a series of determining right and wrong answers, and standardized tests favor the convergent thinker. But when we pursue only convergent-rich curricula, we miss the equally vital arena of divergent thinking.

Is Divergent Thinking Different?
Yes! Divergent thinking encourages your child's mind to explore many possible solutions—maybe even ideas that aren't necessarily apparent at first. It is in use when he discovers that there is more than one way to build a bridge with blocks, to animate a movie, or even to complete a doodle. Radically different from read-and-regurgitate textbooks, not only are divergent activities intellectually stimulating, but kids love them too.

Make a Conscious Effort to Include Both in Your Curriculum

Admittedly, because most textbooks and even puzzles are designed for convergent thinking, you will need to make a conscious effort to expose your children to multiple opportunities for divergent thinking. This is imperative because both divergent and convergent thinking are necessary for critical thinking to be effective.

Why Doctors Need Both Skills

As an example, let's look at a medical doctor. A physician needs to be extraordinarily skilled at convergent thinking to dose medications correctly, diagnose life-threatening emergencies, and follow safety procedures to avoid infection.

However, the first person to wash his hands before surgery or to find a treatment for Ebola used divergent thinking. They were thinking outside of the usual box to solve the problem.

Some of the best doctors today are those who employ powerful convergent skills to accurately diagnose, paired with curiosity and divergent thinking to find the most effective or previously undiscovered treatment plans.

Practical Tips for Tiny Ones

A smart way to implement both convergent and divergent learning at this age is as simple as varying what you ask. If you ask your toddler to make a tower identical to yours, you're asking him a question with only one right answer, so that's a convergent skill.

To make it divergent, ask him to build you a tower as tall as yours or one that uses the same colors. Now you've taken the same idea and added a divergent element. Just keep in mind that he needs both, and you'll be off and running!

Sensory Bins

What Are They? And Why Bother?

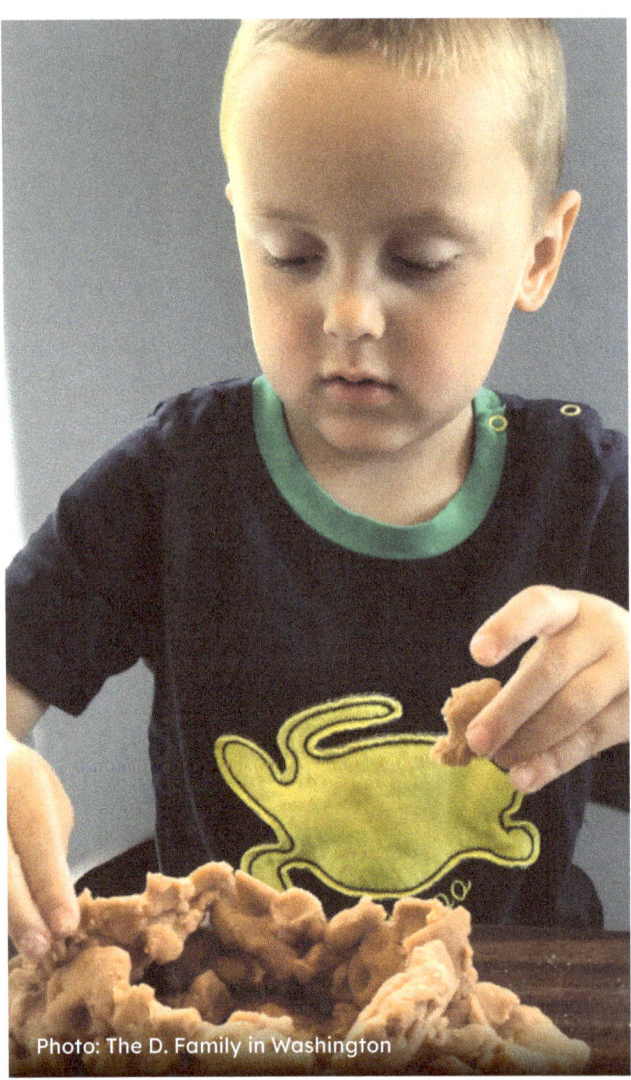

Photo: The D. Family in Washington

If you're an Instagrammer, you've probably seen eye-catching sensory bins scroll across your screen. As parents of young children, this is a case where we actually find a fad somewhat helpful.

What Is a Sensory Bin?

A sensory bin usually exists around a theme and includes both filler and props. Filler can be such things as:

- rice
- noodles
- water
- Mad Mattr (a personal favorite)
- kinesthetic sand
- snow
- gravel
- play dough
- oobleck (cornstarch + water)
- instant snow
- shaving cream
- sand
- kitchen ingredients (like baking soda)
- cereal

Props may include measuring cups, toy animals, small trucks, funnels, Duplo people...the sky is the limit!

Is This a New Thing?

No! Our parents did "sensory bins" by letting us splash around scrubbing pots in the sink, making mud pies in the yard, or playing with our spaghetti at our high chairs.

Why Bother?

Children desperately need sensory experiences. These by no means need to be put into a bin or set apart from real life, but if it is challenging for you to provide the input they need in the natural rhythms of life, a sensory bin approach can be a lifesaver.

Our crew is long on sensory challenges, and we are short on time. So we often find that pulling out a sensory bin provides the moment of calm both of us need.

Of course, this need not be fancy! A bowl of soapy water and some measuring cups are more popular around here than a commercial play-dough kit, but we use both.

What If I Don't Have the Right Ingredients?

Tweak it! Use what you have. Perhaps you have a newly walking toddler who will eat anything. This may be the time to convert your stale cereal into dump truck filler, leftover cooked dinner rice into snow fields in Antarctica, etc.

What Skills Will My Child Learn?

Obviously this will vary with the choices you make in assembling the bin.

Here are some skills we've seen our crew learning:

- pouring
- independent play
- gripping
- regulation
- focus
- coordination
- cause and effect
- persistence
- more vs. less
- empathy
- sharing

Each of these is truly a skill worth pursuing. How much more when the activity is a fun one that engages your child while you feed the baby—or allows you to play along and create some special memories together!

Tips

Some children may need to learn to play independently. If that's true for your child, consider setting a timer and asking him to play for 10 minutes before moving on.

If your child can't sit still for reading time, consider having him play with his sensory bin while you read.

Workbooks as Blank Walls

And Other Reasons to Use Workbooks with Your Little Guys

When we talk about workbooks for the 5-and-under crowd, we almost always hear the same thing from certain folks. They thoughtfully respond, "He's a little young for worksheets. Don't push him into academics this young, but instead just let him 'be a kid' for now." We beg to differ!

Of course, let's not forget to state the obvious. We agree 100% that there really isn't a push to get a young child enjoying workbooks. After all, we are not here to build a child genius whose incredible academic success was obtained at the expense of his joyful spirit and creative personality, or worse yet, to advocate that you gear his education around what makes you look great as his parents.

Workbooks Are Blank Walls!

Don't forget, though, that your child already loves to create. If you doubt that, give him free rein with markers and watch his masterpiece emerge on the walls! So what's the difference between the walls and a workbook for him? How do we get him excited about the potential on his page? Not every child is reluctant to engage with a worksheet for the same reason. Here are a few of the most common scenarios we've seen.

The Overwhelmed Student

Some children are honestly just dismayed by the idea of a worksheet or sitting down to work on a workbook page. Our friends have a child who loved everything about worksheets but initially freaked out at the idea of sitting down and working on them. (This is typically an oldest-child phenomenon, as younger siblings are almost always eager to have their own workbooks just like their older siblings!) For this type of child, it may be helpful to find some pages that you know he will enjoy once he relaxes and to work through one a day as a nonoptional activity. The point isn't to force him to do something too advanced for him but to help him overcome his fears so that he can enjoy this new activity.

The On-and-Off-the-Chair Child

Some children—especially boys or those with sensory processing challenges—don't have the attention span or physical ability to sit still or hold a pencil for long enough to do a page. If that's your child, I'd suggest almost the same approach as for the overwhelmed child but for entirely different reasons. If he has one quick page to do and then is off and running again, he will begin to build the muscle memory and attention span he needs without burdening him now with page after page of seatwork. There is a fine line between forcing him to do something too difficult and helping him build skills. You know him well enough to know exactly what that balance is. Pushing for a tiny bit of growth each week will help him develop skills and endurance that leave him free to create and explore!

The I-Don't-Get-the-Point Kid

Most children are naturally curious and will love solving problems on paper. However, some will do so much better if you take a moment to make a story about the page. Is today's activity drawing lines from birds to nests? Perhaps these could be "busy mommy birds that went and caught food for baby [child's name] but now can't find their way back home. Can you draw a line to help each mommy get home? The baby birds are SO hungry!" Simple? Yes, but extremely engaging to the story-driven child!

Tip 1: Start Short and Sweet

This is a workout for him, and you're not going to begin with a marathon. Just have him do 1 page (or less) of the type he finds most interesting. Ideally, do it just before the best part of his day. If he knows that as soon as he's done you're off to the park, it will help him focus.

Tip 2: Work Through It

Be prepared to take much longer than it "should" to get his work done the first week. Some children may even benefit from hand-over-hand assistance to get the hang of how doable this is. We're not talking about spending hours at the table, but don't expect the 2-minute page to take only 2 minutes the first time!

Tip 3: Make It Amazing

Take another look at your supplies and worksheets. Do the markers make a horrid screeching noise as they grate across the page? Are the worksheets only covering things he already knows? Or are they perhaps just way too hard for him?

Tip 4: Don't Forget the Goal

You know that once he can enjoy worksheets, he is going to love creating and exploring in ways he can't do without them. At the same time, very few skills are limited to worksheets only. Pencil grip can be encouraged by using Mad Mattr. Math will be introduced with manipulatives, and language arts will be naturally encouraged with endless reading times. So don't be overwhelmed by the learning process here—figure out what works best for your family and do that. We just want to encourage you not to throw out workbooks for little guys entirely. Done right, they add so much fun to these younger years!

I Need a Homeschool Group, Right?

Community vs. Co-ops and More

No doubt you're familiar with some homeschool curricula that demand that their families form a group, take turns teaching, and meet weekly to press forward together. You may even wonder why you don't see pop-up Timberdoodle groups across the country/world.

This is a great question! The answer is very simple. You don't need one. Timberdoodle kits stand alone and are not teacher-intensive, meaning you can do it yourself and likely will!

Setting Your Own Pace—The Good

If you customized your kit at all, or if you have adjusted your schedule to your own life, it will make sense to you that your child does not need to be bound to any other child's progress. This is a huge goal of homeschooling: untether your child to proceed at precisely his own pace.

Setting Your Own Pace—The Bad

However, completely isolating yourself from other homeschoolers is far from ideal as well. You may not realize that the attention-span issues you are experiencing are completely age-appropriate or that it is atypical for your first-grader to be unable to follow a story without a lot of help.

Perhaps more importantly, there is a bit of good peer pressure for you in the form of community. If you are a relaxed "we'll do that next week" kind of person, it may be extremely helpful to have a friend asking you if you ever did get around to it and how it went.

Setting Your Own Pace—The Ugly

We are designed for community, and without it, the ugly side shows. From families who seem to care only about themselves to children who don't know how to interact with others, isolation is challenging on many fronts. COVID has certainly highlighted that for all of us!

We need each other, and we need to be deeply in each other's lives in order to flourish.

So Should I Start a Homeschool Group?

You could. And it could be lovely! But first take a look at your goals. Here are some that might apply:

- spend time with people I respect
- invest in others (Kids in your community? Parents who could use a mentor?)
- engage my kids with people who are different from them
- learn some skills
- have friends in real life, not just on social media
- team up for the parts of homeschooling I find stressful
- be encouraged to read widely
- get outside more

So many more ideas could be added! What things do you hope for this year, outside of finishing the materials in your kit? Once you know your goals, pick a format that works well for you and get the ball rolling.

Community Starters

- Start a group that meets at a different local park every Tuesday at noon. Pack lunch and enjoy some time with local moms and kids. Make a group text or other low-key way to make sure everyone knows they are welcome and knows which weeks are where.
- Join a local Facebook group that hosts several kid-friendly hikes a month. Participate those you can.
- Capitalize on P.E. and set aside time and money for ballet class, karate, or swim lessons this year.
- Find your local therapeutic riding / hippotherapy program and see if your horse-crazy teens could volunteer as sidewalkers.
- Google your child's interests. Is there a cooking class you could take together? Perhaps a theater club is starting, or a robotics camp?
- Don't despair if you, like us, find yourself limited by the ages or special needs of your children. A Zoom book study scheduled for after the children are in bed might be just the community you need.
- Buddy up! Look for opportunities for your children to serve. Can they help first-graders practice reading? Assist in after-school programming down the street? Take art or cookies to the local nursing home or shut-in every week? Assist a widow with yard work on Friday afternoons? Your opportunities will vary widely based on your children's ages and abilities, along with local needs. But this is well worth thinking through!
- If you've been involved with the foster care system, you know how critical and yet how draining it can be. Can you team up with a local family to bring lunch once a week and hang out with the kids for a few hours? Or could your teens go help teach younger children a skill? We had a teen come over each week to teach our little girls ballet. Not only is her relationship a huge investment in the girls' lives, but the fact that she comes here is a tremendous blessing as we juggle our erratic schedules and more medically complex little ones.
- Or, if you are that foster family, could you invite a local lonely grandmother-type to join you right in the crazy mess every Monday afternoon for art or reading time?
- Feel like you really need some accountability this year? Ask a friend if she'd be willing to go through your weekly checklists with you each Saturday morning and help you grow in your teaching skills / consistency.
- Make Thursday your Friends & Soup Night and have a standing invitation for friends to join you when possible.

Principles to Keep in Mind

If you're going to set a goal (e.g., get outside more with others), make a specific plan for doing that. (We will take a walk every morning at 9:00, and we will invite families A, B, and C to join us and invite their friends whenever they can.)

You aren't looking for perfection. You won't be able to meet every single week or complete every project you start. Don't panic if you're missing your walk this week because the baby has a doctor appointment or if you woke up with a cold and need to cancel swimming today. But if you make that your exception rather than your norm, you will see tremendous growth this year!

We all need community, but what it "should" look like in each family is something for you to decide, not us. Choose your adventure and get started. We suspect you'll find it is an amazing part of your routine!

The Reading Challenge

Reading Challenge Questions & Answers

Practical Details to Set Up a Productive Routine

So you love the idea of the reading challenge, but you'd like a boost to get you started? You've come to the right place!

Customize This!

You'll find a few ideas here for each challenge, but don't forget that you're not bound to our list. There are literally hundreds more options that may be even better for your family. Use these pages as starter ideas, not as your final list.

Will I See the Same Books Over and Over?

You might see some books repeated, but not too often. Each grade has its own set of books to read, so most books won't show up in multiple places, though about 25% might appear in more than one grade. This happens if a book fits really well in different challenges.

However, many books within your grade could fit into more than one category, but we only list them in one place within your challenges to make it easier for you. So if you want to read more than one book from a certain challenge, you'll probably find another challenge that fits the book if you skim through the list.

Photo: The Coulter Family in New Jersey

A Variety of Reading Levels

As you probably guessed, these are a mix of books to read to your child and books that he will read himself. Read-alouds meet your child's tremendous need for literacy, language, and stories, giving him a strong sense of why he wants to learn to read.

Notes about Our Book Ideas

If you've been reading to your child long (or if you've perused your local public library), you've probably noticed that families have very different standards for their reading materials. The books we've listed here are ones that members of our team have read, have added to their "I want to read this" list, or have had recommended to them.

Even among our team there is a wide range in what titles our families would find acceptable. Some of us find fantasy objectionable but will gladly read a scarier adventure story than other families would be comfortable with. Others of us consider those fantasy titles to be an interesting addition and worthy of much discussion!

Similarly, some of us prefer to avoid titles with troublesome language, bad attitudes, or other concerns, while others prefer to read and discuss them. We've opted to include titles with abandon, knowing that you can flip through them at the library to determine if they are a good fit for your family.

This is not a "Timberdoodle would sell these books if we could" list. We can't vouch for each of the titles, and we certainly can't know which ones are a good fit for your particular family. We even include titles with things we don't like, knowing that what is a "burn the book" moment for one family is a discussion starter for others. And if ever there was a time for deep discussion around many topics, this is that time!

We also are not above editing on the fly. If a book will be helpful for our kids except for a particular line, we'll often edit that line out as we read aloud. This would likely be a poor solution for permanent bookshelf residents, but it's perfect for library books!

Mostly we're providing this list to give you some ideas, just in case you're drawing a blank in thinking of books for a particular topic. Use these ideas as the jumping-off point for which they are intended, and, as always, we highly recommend previewing the books yourself.

Use Your Library

We can't overemphasize how useful your local library will be to you this year. Now that most libraries allow you to place books on hold online, you'll find that you can use any spare hour in your day to request books for the next challenges, and then whoever is in town next can swing by the library and pick them up. If you've not yet become a dedicated library user, start now!

When we checked, roughly half of these books were available in some format from our local library. Since each library's selection varies, we've opted to keep them all listed here knowing that your selection will be different from ours.

If you have Kindle Unlimited or Everand, you will have still another library to choose from.

Reading and Talking

If you're newer to reading together, our biggest tips for you are these. First, just read together. Whether you read through one book a month or several a day, you are making memories and enjoying stories together.

Second, make sure you're discussing what you're reading. This doesn't need to be a formal book report on every book you encounter (please no!) or a tedious question-and-answer session every evening. Instead, talk as you go about the character qualities you see displayed, the kindnesses done (and undone), and the problems being solved. What does your child like about the book? What would he change if he could? If he was a character, which one would he be?

Simple questions build connection, emotional intelligence, worldview, logic, observational skills, and so much more.

Photo: The Panakkal Family in Texas

Reading and Racism

It is worth noting that many of the books we grew up on have terrible racist undertones (e.g., the neighbor in *Little House on the Prairie* who announces that "the only good Indian is a dead Indian" or those Tintin titles which portray people of color in negative ways). We have kept some of these titles on our reading list because racism is a crucial issue to discuss thoughtfully with your child, rather than just pretending it doesn't exist.

What Can You Do: Teaching Your Family To Be Anti-Racist by Tasha

Being anti-racist requires intentional and continuous action on your part as a mom. You set the tone for your home. Your children see what you truly value and believe. Waiting for "the right time" or when your child is "old enough" will be too late.

1. Point out racism in movies and literature. Classics especially. Think *Little House on the Prairie for a minute. Dr. Seuss*. To Kill a Mockingbird. Adventures of Huckleberry Finn. *I am not saying don't have these books on your shelves, but I am saying read them with your child and discuss why the author depicted the People of Color in those negative or rude ways.*

2. Discuss hard stuff. You should always be explicit with children, of all ages, that racism is very hurtful and always wrong. Teach your child to be an ally. Teach them to speak up when they hear someone saying racist comments or jokes. Teach them to be a friend to the refugees, the low-income kids, the disabled kids, the Hispanic kids, etc., etc.

3. Diversify your shelves. Find books and movies about People of Color, preferably where the storyline isn't about diversity. Continuously expose your child to the beauty and richness of the world—the peoples, cultures, religions, buildings, fashions, and foods. Watch the hard things. Read hard books. Don't shy away from the hard conversations.

4. Don't make racist jokes. Period. Racist jokes are so hurtful because they are basically saying, "You are so far beneath me, I can both conceal and express my prejudice and you can't do anything about it because it's socially acceptable—it's 'only' a joke."

We've quoted Tasha (previously a Timberdoodle blogger) here with her permission. Thank you, Tasha!

Reading and Gender Bias

Have you ever reflected that girls are commonly expected to enjoy books with both male and female protagonists, while boys are told that books featuring girls are "girl books" and unworthy of their attention? (Want to read up on this? See the thought-provoking book *A Place to Belong* by Amber O'Neal Johnston.)

I'm not talking about following interests here. By all means your dragon lover should enjoy books on dragons and your artsy person will appreciate books detailing technique. (And in our household it is a girl who loves the dragon books and a boy who is a particularly gifted artist.)

So what do I mean? Don't relegate books with female heroes to the girls' shelves. Just as girls enjoy books with male heroes, boys can and should enjoy books featuring female heroines. Enjoy each book for its content and teach your boys that yes, girls (and their stories) matter and are worthy of their time and attention.

Make This List Even Better

We love your book recommendations and feedback! Did you find a book you loved this year? We'd love to add your recommendations! Just shoot us a note at books@timberdoodle.com and let us know. Or were you perhaps disenchanted with one of our suggestions? Please let us know!

At the end of the year, fill out the Book Awards page near the end of this handbook and submit that. We'll be thrilled to credit you 50 Doodle Dollar reward points (worth $2.50 off your next order) as our thank-you for taking the time to share.

Tracking Your Reading Challenge

Can You Completely Fill This In?

If you're doing the topics out of order, check off completed topics as you go, and you'll be able to tell at a glance which topics are left. Across the page, color in one book after completing each week's reading to see your progress through the challenge at a glance. You can also record your book choices using the chart on each topic's page. If you prefer a printable version of the progress tracker please visit your Timberdoodle.com account for your printable download. You can even print it poster-sized! (Ordered through a school district? Contact us with your order number, and we'll get you set up!)

Reading Challenge Topics

Babies	☐	Opposites	☐
Fruits and Vegetables	☐	Playing	☐
Words	☐	Weather	☐
Nursery Rhymes	☐	Shapes	☐
Helping	☐	Love	☐
Fall	☐	Bathtime	☐
Out and About	☐	Birthdays	☐
Home	☐	Spring	☐
Things That Go	☐	Backyard	☐
Music	☐	Pets	☐
Mealtime	☐	Numbers	☐
Growing Up	☐	Feelings	☐
Farm	☐	Toys	☐
Colors	☐	Space	☐
Animal Babies	☐	Bedtime	☐
Clothes	☐	Mommies and Daddies	☐
Social Skills	☐	Ocean	☐
Winter	☐	Summer	☐

Babies

Challenge 1

All about Me! by Dawn Sirett (DK Baby Sparkle)
Babies by Gyo Fujikawa (So Tall Board Books)
Babies Around the World by Puck
Baby Dear by Esther and Eloise Wilkin (Little Golden Book)
Baby Faces by Jim Harbison (Little Grasshopper)
Baby Faces by Kate Merritt (Indestructibles)
Baby Faces Peekaboo! by Dawn Sirett (DK Peekaboo!)
Baby Says by John Steptoe
Baby Says Peekaboo! by Dawn Sirett (DK Peekaboo!)
Baby's First Book by Garth Williams (Little Golden Book)
Baby's Very First Black and White Book: Babies (Usborne)
Biscuit and the Baby by Alyssa Satin Capucilli (I Can Read)
Brown Sugar Baby by Kevin Lewis
Cat's First Baby by Natalie Nelson
Dog's First Baby by Natalie Nelson
Everywhere Babies by Susan Meyers
Global Babies (Global Fund for Children)
Hello, Baby! (Ladybird Baby Touch)
Hooray for Babies! by Susan Meyers
Look at You! (Star Bright Books)
Look! Babies Head to Toe by Robie H. Harris
My New Baby by Rachel Fuller
Peekaboo Baby by Camilla Reid
Ten Little Fingers and Ten Little Toes by Mem Fox
Ten Tiny Toes by Caroline Jayne Church
Uh-Oh! by Shutta Crum
Welcome, Baby by Natalia Kyle (Little Hippo)
Welcome, Baby by Stephan Lomp (Indestructibles)
Welcome, Baby! A Lift-the-Flap Book for New Babies by Karen Katz
Where's Baby's Belly Button? by Karen Katz
Wonderful Babies by Emily Winfield Martin

	The Book You Chose	**Date Completed**
1.1 *Light Reader*		
1.2 *Interested Reader*		
1.3 *Avid Reader*		
1.4 *Committed Reader*		
1.5 *Enthralled Reader*		

Fruits & Vegetables
Challenge 2

5 Little Apples by Yusuke Yonezu
A Is for Artichoke by Maddie Frost
Apples by Gail Gibbons
Apples, Apples by Kathleen Weidner Zoehfeld
Apples, Apples, Apples by Nancy Elizabeth Wallace
Banana for Two by Ellen Mayer
The Carrot Seed by Ruth Krauss
Carrot Soup by Oakley Graham (Little Hippo)
Counting Peas by Rosemary Wells (Baby Max and Ruby)
Dining Dinosaurs by Chloe Marie (Little Hippo)
Eat 'Em Up Apples by Gail Tuchman
Eat 'Em Up Bananas by Gail Tuchman
Eat 'Em Up Oranges by Gail Tuchman
Eat 'Em Up Pears by Gail Tuchman
Eat Your Colors by Amanda Miller (Rookie Toddler)
Eating the Alphabet: Fruits and Vegetables from A to Z by Lois Ehlert
Fruits and Colors: An English-Spanish Bilingual Book for Babies and Toddlers by Kathleen Motoa
Goodnight, Veggies by Diana Murray
Guess What? - Fruit by Yusuke Yonezu
How Do Apples Grow? by Jill McDonald (Hello, World)
I Like Fruit by Lorena Simonovich (Petit Collage)
I Like Vegetables by Lorena Siminovich (Petit Collage)
Lift and Look Fruits and Vegetables by Tracy Cottingham
Mrs. Peaknuckle's Fruit Alphabet
Mrs. Peaknuckle's Vegetable Alphabet
My First Book of Fruits (Wonder House Books)
My First Book of Vegetables (Wonder House Books)
Orange Pear Apple Bear by Emily Gravett
Pat the Bunny: At the Apple Orchard by Luis Vilela
Peekaboo Apple by Camilla Reid (Nosy Crow)
Red Apple, Green Pear: A Book of Colors (Rookie Toddler)
Red Pepper, Yellow Squash: A Book of Colors (Rookie Toddler)
Strawberries Are Red by Petr Horacek
Superhero Foods (Little Hippo)
Taste the Fruit! by Lizzy Doyle (Indestructibles)
The Very Berry Counting Book by Jerry Pallotta
You're the Apple of My Pie by Rose Rossner (Punderland)

	The Book You Chose	**Date Completed**
2.1 *Light Reader*		
2.2 *Interested Reader*		
2.3 *Avid Reader*		
2.4 *Committed Reader*		
2.5 *Enthralled Reader*		

First Words
Challenge 3

100 First Words (Tiger Tales)
1,000 Useful Words: Build Vocabulary and Literacy Skills (DK)
ABC by Xavier Deneux (Think Touch Learn)
ABC Baby Signs by Christiane Engel
Alphablock by Christopher Franceschelli
Babies Love First Words by Scarlett Wing (Chunky Lift-a-Flap)
Baby Babble by Kate Merritt (Indestructibles)
Baby Pig Pig Talks by David McPhail
Baby Signs by Joy Allen
Baby's First Words by Jim Harbison and Ann Taylor
Baby's Words by Bettina Paterson (So Tall Board Books)
Classic Lit A to Z by Jennifer Adams (BabyLit)
Colorful First Words by Scott Barker (Little Hippo)
First 100 Words by Roger Priddy
First 101 Words: A Highlights Hide-and-Seek Book with Flaps
First Words (DK Baby Sparkle)
First Words (DK Baby Touch and Feel)
First Words (DK Pop-Up Peekaboo)
First Words (DK Sophie La Girafe)
First Words (Poke-a-Dot)
First Words by Roger Priddy (Alphaprints)
Gotta Go, Buffalo by Haily and Kevin Meyers
Let's Sign, Baby! by Kelly Ault
My First 100 Neighborhood Words by Maggie Testa (Daniel Tiger's Neighborhood)
My First Baby Signs by Phil Conigliaro and Tae Won Yu
My First Book of ABC (Wonder House Books)
My First Signs by Annie Kubler
My First Words: Baby's Handbook by Amy Johnson
Peek-a-Flap Words by Jaye Garnett
Poppy and Sam's First Word Book by Sam Taplin (Usborne)
Richard Scarry's Best Little Word Book Ever (Little Golden Book)
Very First Book of Things to Spot (Usborne)
What Does Baby Say? A Lift-the-Flap Book by Karen Katz
Where's Baby? by Anne Hunter
Words (DK My First)
Words by Roger Priddy (Bright Baby Touch and Feel)
Wordy Birdy by Tammi Sauer

	The Book You Chose	**Date Completed**
3.1 *Light Reader*		
3.2 *Interested Reader*		
3.3 *Avid Reader*		
3.4 *Committed Reader*		
3.5 *Enthralled Reader*		

Nursery Rhymes

Challenge 4

5 Minute Nursery Rhymes (Tiger Tales)
Ditty Bird Nursery Rhymes
Eric Carle's Twinkle, Twinkle, Little Star and Other Nursery Rhymes
Favorite Nursery Rhymes from Mother Goose illustrated by Scott Gustafson
Head, Shoulders, Knees and Toes by Yu-hsuan Huang (Sing Along with Me)
Hey Diddle Diddle by Yu-hsuan Huang (Sing Along with Me)
Hey Diddle Diddle by Jonas Sickler (Indestructibles)
Hey Diddle Diddle and Other Nursery Rhymes by Dawn Machell (Stories in Stitches)
Hickory Dickory Dock by Kelly Caswell (Child's Play)
Hickory Dickory Dock by Yu-hsuan Huang (Sing Along with Me)
Hickory Dickory Dock by Jonas Sickler (Indestructibles)
Hickory Dickory Dock: A Collection of Nursery Rhymes (Tiger Tales My Little World)
Hickory Dickory Dock and Other Favorite Nursery Rhymes by Sanja Rescek (Tiger Tales)
Humpty Dumpty by Jonas Sickler (Indestructibles)
Humpty-Dumpty and Other Rhymes by Iona Opie
Itsy Bitsy Spider and Other Nursery Rhymes by Dawn Machell (Stories in Stitches)
Little Miss Muffet by Barbara Nascimbeni (Child's Play)
Mary Engelbreit's Mother Goose
Mother Goose Rhymes by Stacy Peterson (Little Grasshopper)
My First Book of Nursery Rhymes illustrated by Sanja Rescek
My First Real Mother Goose by Blanche Fisher Wright
Nursery Rhymes by Lucy Cousins
Nursery Rhymes by Roger Priddy (Lift the Flap)
Nursery Rhymes: A Mirror Book by Kathrin Fehrl (Little Hippo)
Pat-a-Cake: First Book of Nursery Rhymes by Ailie Busby
Rhyme Book (Ladybird Baby Touch)
Snuggle Up with Mother Goose by Iona Opie
This Little Piggy by Vanja Kragulj (Indestructibles)
This Little Piggy and Other Favorite Action Rhymes by Hannah Wood (Tiger Tales)
This Little Piggy: Touch and Trace Nursery Rhymes by Emily Bannister
Tomie's Little Mother Goose by Tomie DePaola

	The Book You Chose	**Date Completed**
4.1 *Light Reader*		
4.2 *Interested Reader*		
4.3 *Avid Reader*		
4.4 *Committed Reader*		
4.5 *Enthralled Reader*		

Helping

Challenge 5

Bear and Bird Lend a Helping Hand by Jonny Lambert
Big Enough to Help by Becky Friedman (Daniel Tiger's Neighborhood)
Bizzy Bear: Do-It-Yourself Day by Benji Davies (Nosy Crow)
Brownie and Pearl Make Good by Cynthia Rylant
Chores Galore by Marc Mones (Little Hippo)
Chores Outdoors by Marc Mones (Little Hippo)
Clean It! by Georgie Birkett (Helping Hands)
Clean-Up Time by Elizabeth Verdick (Toddler Tools)
Clean-Up Time by Rosemary Wells (Baby Max and Ruby)
Daniel Meets the New Neighbors by Jason Fruchter (Daniel Tiger's Neighborhood)
Friends Help Each Other by Simon Spotlight (Daniel Tiger's Neighborhood)
Helping by Helen Oxenbury
Helping Daddy by Mathew Price

Henry Helps series by Beth Bracken
I Am Helping by Mercer Mayer (Little Critter)
I Help by Cheri J. Meiners
It's the Helpers by Sandra Magsamen (Looky Looky Little One)
Kipper Helps Out by Mick Inkpen
Lend a Helping Paw: A Touch-and-Feel Adventure (PAW Patrol)
Let's Celebrate! Helping by Sophia Day (MVP Kids)
Little Tiger Picks Up by Michael Dahl (Hello Genius)
Llama Llama Mess Mess Mess by Anna Dewdney
Mommy's Big Helper: Touch and Feel by Rufus Downy
My First Toolbox by John Hansen (Little Hippo)
Pat the Bunny: May I Help You? by Edith Kunhardt

	The Book You Chose	**Date Completed**
5.1 *Light Reader*		
5.2 *Interested Reader*		
5.3 *Avid Reader*		
5.4 *Committed Reader*		
5.5 *Enthralled Reader*		

Fall

Challenge 6

Autumn in the Forest by Rusty Finch (Lift-a-Flap)
Baby Loves Fall! A Karen Katz Lift-the-Flap Book
Baby's First Thanksgiving (DK)
Bear's New Friend by Karma Wilson
Biscuit Visits the Pumpkin Patch by Alyssa Satin Capucilli
The Book of Fall by Agnese Baruzzi
The Busy Little Squirrel: A Book About Seasons by Nancy Tafuri
Clifford's First Autumn by Norman Bridwell
Daniel Loves Fall! by Jason Fruchter (Daniel Tiger's Neighborhood)
Daniel Visits a Pumpkin Patch by Maggie Testa (Daniel Tiger's Neighborhood)
Daniel's Apple-Picking Adventure by Maggie Testa (Daniel Tiger's Neighborhood)
Dinosaur, Dinosaur, Fall Is Here and Other Rhymes illustrated by Sanja Rescek (Tiger Tales)
Duck and Goose Find a Pumpkin by Tad Hills
Duck, Duck, Dinosaur: Perfect Pumpkin by Kallie George (I Can Read)
Fall by Chris Demarest
Fall Is Here! by Fhiona Galloway
Fun Fall Day: A Touch and Feel Book by Tara Knudson
Here Comes Fall! by Susan Kantor
I Love Fall! A Touch-and-Feel Board Book by Allison Inches
Leaves by David Ezra Stein
Leaves! Leaves! Leaves! by Nancy Elizabeth Wallace
Little Pumpkin by Gisela Bohorquez (Nature Stories)
Mouse's First Fall by Lauren Thompson
My Autumn Book by Wong Herbert Yee
Night Night, Pumpkin by Amy Parker
Now It's Fall by Lois Lenski
Penguin and Pumpkin by Salina Yoon
The Poky Little Puppy and the Pumpkin Patch by Diane Muldrow (Little Golden Book)
Pumpkin Day! by Nancy Elizabeth Wallace
Touch and Feel Fall (Scholastic Early Learners)
The Very Hungry Caterpillar's First Fall by Eric Carle
Welcome Fall by Jill Ackerman (Little Scholastic)
What Is Fall? by Genie Espinosa

	The Book You Chose	**Date Completed**
6.1 *Light Reader*		
6.2 *Interested Reader*		
6.3 *Avid Reader*		
6.4 *Committed Reader*		
6.5 *Enthralled Reader*		

Out & About

Challenge 7

At the Zoo by Roger Priddy (Bright Baby Touch and Feel)
Baby Goes Shopping by Monica Wellington
Baby's First Around Town by Scott Barker (Teaching Tots)
Baby's Very First Black and White Book: Going Out (Usborne)
Bear About Town by Stella Blackstone
Biscuit Takes a Walk by Alyssa Satin Capucilli (I Can Read)
Bizzy Bear: Fun Park by Benji Davies (Nosy Crow)
Bizzy Bear: Let's Go and Play! by Benji Davies (Nosy Crow)
Brownie & Pearl Step Out by Cynthia Rylant
Busy City by Maddie Frost (Indestructibles)
Busy Funfair by Rebecca Finn (Busy Books)
Busy Park (Campbell Books)
Busy Park by Rebecca Finn (Busy Books)
Busy Shopping (Campbell Books)
Busy Town by Rebecca Finn (Busy Books)
Busy Zoo by Ruth Redford (Campbell Books)
Calm at the Restaurant by Jason Fruchter (Daniel Tiger's Neighborhood)
Cityblock by Christopher Franceschelli
Corduroy's Neighborhood by Don Freeman
Curious George's Neighborhood by Margret and H.A. Rey
Everyday Town by Cynthia Rylant
Hurry, Hurry, Little Sloth by Joe Rhatigan (Little Hippo)
Lois Looks for Bob at the Park by Gerry Turley (Nosy Crow)
Mrs. Peaknuckle's Earth Alphabet
Mrs. Peaknuckle's Hiking Alphabet
My Neighborhood by Maddie Frost (Indestructibles)
Night Night, Sleepytown by Amy Parker
On the Go! by Ailie Busby
On-the-Go Time by Elizabeth Verdick (Toddler Tools)
Out and About (DK My First)
Playtown: A Lift-the-Flap Book by Roger Priddy
Shopping by Rosemary Wells (Baby Max and Ruby)
Sign About Going Out by Anthony Lewis (Child's Play)
Twins in the Park by Ellen Weiss (Ready to Read)
Very First Book of Things to Spot Out and About (Usborne)

	The Book You Chose	**Date Completed**
7.1 *Light Reader*		
7.2 *Interested Reader*		
7.3 *Avid Reader*		
7.4 *Committed Reader*		
7.5 *Enthralled Reader*		

Home

Challenge 8

At Home by Agnese Baruzzi (Baby's First Library)
Baby's First Words: Home by Lesley Grainger (Bloomsbury)
Bear at Home by Stella Blackstone
Bears on Chairs by Shirley Parenteau
Cows in the Kitchen by Airlie Anderson (Child's Play)
Everyday House by Cynthia Rylant
Home for a Bunny by Margaret Wise Brown (Little Golden Book)
Home Sweet Home by Roger Priddy (Little Friends)
Home Sweet Home by Stephan Lomp (Indestructibles)
Home, Sweet Home with Touch and Feel Flaps! (Make Believe Ideas)
Lois Looks for Bob at Home by Gerry Turley (Nosy Crow)
Maisy at Home: A First Words Book by Lucy Cousins
Mrs. Peaknuckle's Kitchen Alphabet
My First Book of Things at Home (Wonder House Books)

New House by Dave Wheeler
Peekaboo House by Camilla Reid (Nosy Crow)
Shapes at Home (Rookie Toddler)
Ten Little Monkeys Jumping on the Bed by Annie Kubler
This Is the House That Jack Built by Pam Adams
Very First Book of Things to Spot at Home (Usborne)
We Are Friends at Home by Sue Downing (DK)
Welcome Home, Bear: A Book of Animal Habitats by Il Sung Na
What's in My House? by Roger Priddy (Slide and Find)

	The Book You Chose	**Date Completed**
8.1 *Light Reader*		
8.2 *Interested Reader*		
8.3 *Avid Reader*		
8.4 *Committed Reader*		
8.5 *Enthralled Reader*		

Things That Go

Challenge 9

Babies Love Things That Go by Scarlett Wing
The Babies on the Bus by Karen Katz
Baby Go! Go! Go! (DK Baby Sparkle)
Big and Little Things That Go (Rookie Toddler)
Bizzy Bear: Airplane Pilot by Benji Davies (Nosy Crow)
Bizzy Bear: Off We Go! by Benji Davies (Nosy Crow)
Bizzy Bear: Race Car Driver by Benji Davies (Nosy Crow)
Bizzy Bear: Train Engineer by Benji Davies (Nosy Crow)
Brownie and Pearl Go for a Spin by Cynthia Rylant
Busy Airport (Campbell Books)
Busy Airport by Rebecca Finn (Busy Books)
Busy Cars (Campbell Books)
Busy Garage by Rebecca Finn (Busy Books)
Busy Railroad by Rebecca Finn (Busy Books)
Busy Trains (Campbell Books)
Bye-bye, Train by Pamela Chanko (Rookie Toddler)
Car (Ladybird Baby Touch)
Cars and Trucks by Jill McDonald (Hello, World)
Construction Vehicles (Poke-a-Dot)
Down by the Station by Jess Stockham (Child's Play)
Emergency Vehicles (Poke-a-Dot)
Find It: Things That Go (Highlights)
Fire Engine (DK Baby Touch and Feel)
First 100 Trucks and Things That Go by Roger Priddy
Go, Go, Go! by Bob Barner (I Like to Read)
Go, Go, Go, Dinosaur! by Sam P. Leon (Little Hippo)
Good Night Dump Truck by Adam Gamble
Good Night, Planes by Adam Gamble
Good Night, Trains by Adam Gamble
Happy Baby: Things That Go by Roger Priddy
Little Orange Truck: Country Lift-a-Flap by Ginger Swift
The Little School Bus by Margery Cuyler (Little Vehicles)
My Blue Boat by Chris Demarest
My First Book of Transport (Wonder House Books)
My First Things That Go (DK)
Night Night, Train by Amy Parker
Night Night Truck by Roger Priddy
Noisy Trains by Roger Priddy (Bright Baby)
On the Go by Roger Priddy (Lift-the-Flap Tab Books)
Open the Garage Door... by Christopher Santoro (Lift-the-Flap)
Plane or Boat? by Lenka Cytilova (First Words: Vehicles)
Planes and Other Flying Machines by Jill McDonald
Things That Go (DK Baby Sparkle)
Things That Go (DK Baby Touch and Feel)
Things That Go (DK Pop-Up Peekaboo)
Things That Go by Stephan Lomp (Indestructibles)
Things That Go by Sandra Magsamen (Looky Looky Little One)
Toot Toot Beep Beep by Emma Garcia (All About Sounds)
Train by Chris Demarest
Transportation by Emmy Kastner (Nerdy Babies)
Trucks by Roger Priddy (Lift-the-Flap Tab Books)
Vehicles (Ladybird Baby Touch)
Vehicles by Agnese Baruzzi (Baby's First Library)
Vehicles by Xavier Deneux (Touch Think Learn)
Vroom Things That Go by Scott Barker (Little Hippo)
Vroom, Vroom, Trucks! A Karen Katz Lift-the-Flap Book
What's in My Truck? by Roger Priddy (Slide and Find)
Wheels on the Bus by Sarah Grateley (Little Hippo)
The Wheels on the Bus Go Round and Round by Annie Kubler
The Wheels on the Truck Go 'Round and 'Round (Rookie Toddler)
Zoom, Zoom, Baby! A Karen Katz Lift-the-Flap Book

	The Book You Chose	**Date Completed**
9.1 *Light Reader*		
9.2 *Interested Reader*		
9.3 *Avid Reader*		
9.4 *Committed Reader*		
9.5 *Enthralled Reader*		

Music

Challenge 10

The ABC of Musical Instruments by Ailie Busby
Amazing Me! Music! by Carol Thompson
Baby Shark illustrated by Mike Jackson (Little Golden Book)
Bears in a Band by Shirley Parenteau
Butterfly's Marching Band by Lila Mitzie (Little Hippo)
Charlie Parker Played Be Bop by Chris Raschka
Down by the Bay by Raffi
Five Little Ducks by Penny Ives (Child's Play)
Frere Jacques by Jonas Sickler (Indestructibles)
Happy and You Know It! by Vanja Kragulj (Indestructibles)
Here We Go Round the Mulberry Bush by Annie Kubler
Huff and Puff Sing Along by Tish Rabe (I Can Read)
I Am the Music Man by Debra Potter (Child's Play)
I Love the Mountains illustrated by Haily Meyers
If You're Happy and You Know It by Raffi
If You're Happy and You Know It by Yu-hsuan Huang
Incy Wincy Spider by Yu-hsuan Huang
The Itsy Bitsy Spider by Maddie Frost (Indestructibles)
Jazz Baby by Lisa Wheeler
Jingle Bells by Yu-hsuan Huang (Sing Along with Me)
Koala's Cool Band by Seth A.P. Miller
Mary Had a Little Lamb by Marina Aizen (Child's Play)
Moon River illustrated by Tim Hopgood
Music by Rob Delgaudio (Baby's Big World)
Music by Jill McDonald (Hello, World)
Music Is... by Brandon Stosuy
My First Peter and the Wolf illustrated by Emanuela Di Donna
Old MacDonald Had a Farm by Jane Cabrera
Over in the Meadow by Michael Evans (Child's Play)
Rodgers and Hammerstein's My Favorite Things illustrated by Renee Graef
Row, Row, Row Your Boat by Maddie Frost (Indestructibles)
Row, Row, Row Your Boat by Yu-hsuan Huang
Row, Row, Row Your Boat by Iza Trapani
Singing in the Rain illustrated by Tim Hopgood
The Sound of Music: Do-Re-Mi illustrated by Miriam Bos (Broadway Baby)
The Sound of Music: My Favorite Things illustrated by Daniel Roode (Broadway Baby)
Splat the Cat Sings Flat by Rob Scotton (I Can Read)
Splat the Cat with a Bang and a Clang by Rob Scotton (I Can Read)
The Star-Spangled Banner by Francis Scott Key (Pictureback)
This Old Man by Pam Adams (Child's Play)
Twinkle, Twinkle, Little Star by Maddie Frost (Indestructibles)
Twinkle, Twinkle, Little Star by Yu-hsuan Huang
We Love to Sing Along! by Caroline Jayne Church
What a Wonderful World illustrated by Tim Hopgood
The Wheels on the Bus by James Dean (Pete the Cat)
The Wheels on the Bus by Yu-hsuan Huang
The Wheels on the Bus by Raffi

	The Book You Chose	**Date Completed**
10.1 Light Reader		
10.2 Interested Reader		
10.3 Avid Reader		
10.4 Committed Reader		
10.5 Enthralled Reader		

Mealtime

Challenge 11

Baby, Let's Eat! by Stephan Lomp (Indestructibles)
Baby Signs: All Done! by Kate Lockwood
Baby's First Foods by Scott Barker (Little Hippo)
Bake, Mice, Bake! by Eric Seltzer (Penguin Young Readers)
Busy Baking by Rebecca Finn
Daniel Tries a New Food by Becky Friedman (Daniel Tiger's Neighborhood)
Digger the Dinosaur and the Cake Mistake by Rebecca Kai Dotlich (I Can Read)
Feast for 10 by Cathryn Falwell
Food (Ladybird Baby Touch)
Guess What? – Food by Yusuke Yonezu
I Eat Everything! That's Good for Me by Beth Taylor (Little Grasshopper)
Max's Breakfast by Rosemary Wells (Max and Ruby)
Mealtime (DK Baby Touch and Feel)
Mealtime by Elizabeth Verdick
Munch Your Lunch! by Jason Fruchter (Daniel Tiger's Neighborhood)
Paddington Pancake Day! by Alyssa Satin Capucilli (I Can Read)
Sign about Meal Time by Anthony Lewis
Silly Monsters at Mealtime (Rookie Toddler)
Sip, Chew, Yum: Lift-a-Flap by Scarlett Wing
Snack Time for Cow by Michael Dahl (Hello Genius)
Spot Bakes a Cake by Eric Hill
Stir Crack Whisk Bake by Maddie Frost
The Very Hungry Caterpillar Eats Breakfast by Eric Carle
Yummy! Mealtime: Touch and Feel by Jennifer Schiavello
Yum Yum! by Yusuke Yonezu

	The Book You Chose	**Date Completed**
11.1 *Light Reader*		
11.2 *Interested Reader*		
11.3 *Avid Reader*		
11.4 *Committed Reader*		
11.5 *Enthralled Reader*		

Growing Up
Challenge 12

All by Myself by Aliki
Baby Pig Pig Walks by David McPhail
Big Bed for Giraffe by Michael Dahl (Hello Genius)
Big Bed for Little Bear by Scarlett Wing (I Can Do It)
Bye-Bye Binky by Maria van Lieshout
Bye-Bye Bottles, Zebra by Michael Dahl (Hello Genius)
Come Back, Zack! by Trish Holland (Little Golden Book)
Daniel's Potty Time by Alexandra Cassel Schwartz (Daniel Tiger's Neighborhood)
Diapers Are Not Forever by Elizabeth Verdick (Best Behavior)
Duck Goes Potty by Michael Dahl (Hello Genius)
Everybody Potties! by Cheri Vogel
Going to the Potty by Fred Rogers
I Am Just Right by David McPhail (I Like to Read)
I Can Do It! by Sarah Albee (Step Into Reading)
I Can Do It! by Trish Holland (Little Golden Book)
I Can Do It Too! by Karen Baicker
I Go Potty! (Rookie Toddler)
I'm Not Using the Potty by Laura Gehl (Peep and Egg)
I Sleep in a Big Bed by Maria van Lieshout
I Use the Potty by Maria van Lieshout
I Used to Be the Baby by Robin Ballard
Little by Little by Amber Stewart
Little Red Henry by Linda Urban
Little Juniper Makes It Big by Aiden Cassie
No More Pacifier, Duck by Michael Dahl (Hello Genius)
Now I'm Big! by Karen Katz
Pig Pig Grows Up by David McPhail
A Potty for Me! by Karen Katz
Potty Patrol (Paw Patrol)
Pottysaurus by Brooke Vitale (Little Hippo)
The Prince and the Potty by Wendy Cheyette Lewison
The Princess and the Potty by Wendy Cheyette Lewison
Ruby in Her Own Time by Jonathan Emmett
Thumbs Up, Brown Bear by Michael Dahl (Hello Genius)
Who Says Uh Oh? (Highlights Baby Mirror Board Books)
The Wonderful Things You Will Be by Emily Winfield Martin

	The Book You Chose	**Date Completed**
12.1 *Light Reader*		
12.2 *Interested Reader*		
12.3 *Avid Reader*		
12.4 *Committed Reader*		
12.5 *Enthralled Reader*		

Farm

Challenge 13

123 the Farm and Me by Maddie Frost
At the Farm by Salina Yoon
Babies on the Farm by Ginger Swift
Baby Farm Animals by Ryan Barone (Little Hippo)
Baby's First Farm by Scott Barker (Teaching Tots)
Barnyard Dance! by Sandra Boynton
Big Red Barn by Margaret Wise Brown
Biscuit's Day at the Farm by Alyssa Satin Capucilli (I Can Read)
Busy Farm by Rebecca Finn (Busy Books)
Busy Farmyard by Betina Ogden (So Tall Board Books)
The Busy Little Tractor by Joe Rhatigan (Little Hippo)
Dinosaur, Dinosaur Had a Farm and Other Barnyard Rhymes by Sanja Rescek (Tiger Tales)
Everywhere a Moo, Moo (Rookie Toddler)
Farm by Xavier Deneux (Touch Think Learn)
Farm Animal Families (Poke-a-Dot)
Farm Animal Sounds (Ditty Bird)
Farm Animals by Layla McGrath (Little Hippo)
Farm Counting Adventure: Pop Tales (Little Hippo)
Farm Friends by Jack Redwing (John Deere Kids)
The Farmer in the Dell by Pam Adams (Child's Play)
Find It: Farm (Highlights)
First Farm Words by Roger Priddy
Fun on the Farm by Gareth Lucas (Tiger Tales)
Funny Farm Animals by Connie Whistler (Little Hippo)
Good Night, Farm by Adam Gamble
Hello, Farm! by Maddie Frost (Indestructibles)
Hello, Farm! by Amelia Hepworth (Happy Baby)
In My Barn by Sara Gillingham
Little Red Barn: Farm Lift-a-Flap by Ginger Swift
Lullaby Farm by Stephanie Shaw

Moo Baa La La La! by Sandra Boynton
Moo Moo Peekaboo: A Lift-the-Flap Storybook by Morgan Huff (Little Hippo)
Mornings on the Farm: A Lift-a-Flap Storybook by Claudia Tenorio (Little Hippo)
My First Book of Farm Animals (Wonder House Books)
My First Farm (DK)
Night Night, Farm by Amy Parker
Old MacDonald Had a Farm by Pam Adams (Child's Play)
Old MacDonald Had a Farm by Jonas Sickler (Indestructibles)
Old MacDonald's Farm (Poke-a-Dot)
On the Farm by Jonny Lambert
On the Farm by Jill McDonald (Hello, World)
On the Farm by Sandra Magsamen (Looky Looky Little One)
On the Farm by Roger Priddy (Bright Baby Touch and Feel)
On the Farm: Peek and Seek by Sarah Muthomi
Open the Barn Door... by Christopher Santoro
Peekaboo Cow by Camilla Reid (Nosy Crow)
Peekaboo Farm by Sydnie Wittenberg (Little Hippo)
Peek-a-Flap Moo by Jaye Garnett (Cottage Door Press)
Pigs Don't Pop: Pop Tales (Little Hippo)
Poppy and Sam's Animal Hide and Seek by Stephen Cartwright
Sheep or Cow? by Lenka Chytilova (First Words: Farm)
Spot Goes to the Farm by Eric Hill
Touch and Feel Farm (Scholastic Early Learners)
Tractor (DK Baby Touch and Feel)
Tractor (DK Pop-Up Peekaboo)
Tractor by Amelia Hepworth (How It Works)
Wake Up, Farm! by Jonny Lambert (DK Pop-Up Peekaboo)
Wiggle! March! by Karen Pixton (Indestructibles)
You Are My Baby: Farm by Lorena Siminovich

	The Book You Chose	**Date Completed**
13.1 Light Reader		
13.2 Interested Reader		
13.3 Avid Reader		
13.4 Committed Reader		
13.5 Enthralled Reader		

Colors

Challenge 14

Alice in Wonderland: A BabyLit Colors Primer by Jennifer Adams
Anne's Colors: Inspired by Anne of Green Gables by Kelly Hill
Babies Love Colors by Michelle Rhodes-Conway
Baby, See the Colors! by Ekaterina Trukhan (Indestructibles)
Bear Sees Colors by Karma Wilson (The Bear Books)
Blue Bus, Red Balloon by Brian Biggs (Everything Goes)
Brown Bear, Brown Bear, What Do You See? by Bill Martin Jr.
Can You Find Colors? (Rookie Toddler)
Cat Likes Red by Christopher Russo (I Like to Read)
The Color Kitten by Margaret Wise Brown (Little Golden Book)
Colors (DK Baby Touch and Feel)
Colors (DK My First)
Colors by Jane Conteh-Morgan (So Tall Board Books)
Colors by Xavier Deneux (Touch Think Learn)
Colors by Roger Priddy (Bright Baby Touch and Feel)
Colors Are Nice by Adelaide Holl (Little Golden Book)
The Colors of Summer by Danna Smith (Little Golden Book)
Colours (DK Pop-Up Peekaboo)
Corduroy's Colors by MaryJo Scott
Duck and Goose Colors! by Tad Hills
Dump Truck's Colors by Sherri Duskey Rinker (Goodnight Goodnight Construction Site)
Elmo's Colors by Naomi Kleinberg (Pictureback)
First Book of Colors by Roger Priddy
First Colors (Poke-a-Dot)

Green by Laura Vaccaro Seeger
Happy Baby Colors by Roger Priddy
I Love Pink! by Frances Gilbert (Step Into Reading)
I See Animal Colors (Rookie Toddler)
I Spy with My Little Eye by Edward Gibbs
Jane Foster's Black and White
Kipper's Book of Colors by Mick Inkpen
Learning with Llama Llama: Colors by Anna Dewdney
Little Quack Loves Colors by Lauren Thompson
Mix It Up! by Herve Tullet
My Favorite Book of Colors by Janice Behrens (Rookie Toddler)
My Favorite Color Is... (Rookie Toddler)
My First Book of Colors (Wonder House Books)
New York by Ashley Evanson (Hello World)
One Fish, Two Fish, Red Fish, Blue Fish by Dr. Seuss
Peek-a-Flap Colors by Jaye Garnett
Rainbow (Ladybird Baby Touch)
Rainbow Chameleon by Yusuke Yonezu
Red Car, Green Car by Roger Priddy (A Changing Colors Book)
Spot Goes to the Farm by Eric Hill
Stanley's Colors by William Bee
Tractor Mac Colors the Farm by Billy Steers
Walk and See Colors by Rosalind Beardshaw (Nosy Crow)
What Is Yellow? (Rookie Toddler)
What's Your Favorite Color? (Poke-a-Dot)
White Rabbit's Color Book by Alan Baker

	The Book You Chose	**Date Completed**
14.1 Light Reader		
14.2 Interested Reader		
14.3 Avid Reader		
14.4 Committed Reader		
14.5 Enthralled Reader		

Animal Babies

Challenge 15

Animal Babies by Harry McNaught (Pictureback)
Babies in the Forest by Ginger Swift
Babies in the Wild by Ginger Swift
Babies Love Animals by Scarlett Wing
Baby Animal Friends (DK Baby Sparkle)
Baby Animals (DK My First)
Baby Animals (DK Pop-Up Peekaboo)
Baby Animals by Gyo Fujikawa (So Tall Board Books)
Baby Animals by Anna Jones (Little Hippo)
Baby Animals by Stephan Lomp (Indestructibles)
Baby Animals by Sandra Magsamen (Looky Looky Little One)
Baby Animals by Jill McDonald (Hello, World)
Baby Animals by Roger Priddy (Bright Baby Touch and Feel)
Baby Animals by Garth Williams (Little Golden Book)
Baby Animals on the Farm (Rookie Toddler)
Baby Farm Animals by Garth Williams (Little Golden Book)
Busy Baby Animals by Ag Jatkowska (Busy Books)
Busy Kittens by Samantha Meredith (Busy Books)
Busy Lion Cubs (Busy Books)
Cuddly Animals (DK Baby Touch and Feel)
Everywhere a Moo, Moo (Rookie Toddler)
Fluffy Animals (DK Baby Touch and Feel)
Good Night Baby Animals by Adam Gamble

Happy Baby Animals by Roger Priddy
Hello, Baby Animals! By Amelia Hepworth (Happy Baby)
Kipper's Little Friends by Mick Inkepen
Little Bear by Gina Maldonado (Nature Stories)
Little Foal's Busy Day by Jane Monroe Donovan
A Little Fox by Rosalee Wren
A Little Hedgehog by Rosalee Wren
A Little Piglet by Rosalee Wren
The Littlest Things Give the Loveliest Hugs by Mark Sperring
Mama and Baby! by Kaaren Pixton (Indestructibles)
My First Book of Baby Animals (Wonder House Books)
My Little Wonder: Welcome Sweet Babies by Mack van Gageldonk
Pat the Bunny by Dorothy Kunhardt
Roar! Roar! (DK Baby Touch and Feel)
Springtime Babies by Danna Smith (Little Golden Book)
Touch and Feel Baby Animals (Scholastic Early Learners)
Woodland Babies by Amanda McDonough
Wild Animals (DK Baby Touch and Feel)
Wild Baby by Cori Doerrfeld
You Are My Baby: Meadow by Lorena Siminovich
You Are My Baby: Safari by Lorena Siminovich
You Are My Baby: Woodland by Lorena Siminovich

	The Book You Chose	**Date Completed**
15.1 *Light Reader*		
15.2 *Interested Reader*		
15.3 *Avid Reader*		
15.4 *Committed Reader*		
15.5 *Enthralled Reader*		

Clothes
Challenge 16

Anna Karenina: A BabyLit Fashion Primer by Jennifer Adams
Blue Hat, Green Hat by Sandra Boynton
Brownie and Pearl Get Dolled Up by Cynthia Rylant
Bundle Up by Jennifer Sattler
Caps for Sale by Escphyr Slobodkina
Charlie Needs a Cloak by Tomie de Paola
The Dress I'll Wear to the Party by Shirley Neitzel
Dress Up Peekaboo! (DK)
Fox in Socks by Dr. Seuss (Beginner Books)
Froggy Gets Dressed by Jonathan London
Get Dressed (Ladybird Baby Touch)
Gossie by Olivier Dunrea
The Hat by Jan Brett
A Hat for Minerva Louise by Janet Morgan Stoeke
Hat, Socks, Shoes: Lift-a-Flap by Scarlett Wing
Hats Off to Mr. Pickles! by Sally Lloyd-Jones
Henry Helps with Laundry by Beth Bracken
I Get Dressed by David McPhail
I Had Ten Hats by David McPhail (I Like to Read)
I Love My White Shoes by Eric Litwin (Pete the Cat)
Jesse Bear, What Will You Wear? by Nancy White Carlstrom
Let's Get Dressed by Agnese Baruzzi (Baby's First Library)
Little Sock by Kia Heise and Christopher D. Park
Max's New Suit by Rosemary Wells
The Missing Mitten Mystery by Steven Kellogg
The Mitten by Jan Brett
A New Coat for Anna by Harriet Ziefert
No Red Sweater for Daniel by Becky Friedman (Daniel Tiger's Neighborhood)
Ollie the Stomper by Oliveier Dunrea (Gossie and Friends)
One Red Sock by Jennifer Sattler
Pants for Chuck by Pat Schories (I Like to Read)
Pelle's New Suit by Elsa Beskow
Pete the Cat and His Four Groovy Buttons by Eric Litwin
Pinkalicious: Fashion Fun by Victoria Kann (I Can Read)
Shoes (Rookie Toddler)
What Hat Goes with That? by Pamela Chanko
What Is Daniel Wearing? by Becky Friedman (Daniel Tiger's Neighborhood)
What Shoes Would You Choose? by Pamela Chanko
Whose Hat Is It? by Valeri Gorbachev
Will You Wear a Blue Hat? (Rookie Toddler)

	The Book You Chose	**Date Completed**
16.1 *Light Reader*		
16.2 *Interested Reader*		
16.3 *Avid Reader*		
16.4 *Committed Reader*		
16.5 *Enthralled Reader*		

Social Skills

Challenge 17

123s of Thankfulness by Patricia Hegarty
ABCs of Kindness by Patricia Hegarty
Baby Be Kind by Jane Cowen-Fletcher
Bear and Bird Learn to Share by Jonny Lambert
Bear Says "Thank You" by Michael Dahl (Hello Genius)
But Not the Hippopotamus by Sandra Boynton
Can You Say Please? (Rookie Toddler)
Daniel Goes Out for Dinner by Maggie Testa (Daniel Tiger's Neighborhood)
Feet Are Not for Kicking by Elizabeth Verdick
Germs Are Not for Sharing by Elizabeth Verdick
The Kindness Monster by Marc Mones (Little Hippo)
Let's Be Kind by Ekaterina Trukhan (Indestructibles)
Listening Time by Elizabeth Verdick (Toddler Tools)
Little Dinos Don't Bite by Michael Dahl
Little Dinos Don't Hit by Michael Dahl
Little Dinos Don't Push by Michael Dahl
Little Dinos Don't Yell by Michael Dahl
Little Lion Shares by Michael Dahl (Hello Genius)
Little Turtle Tries by Michael Dahl (Hello Genius)
Llama Llama Time to Share by Anna Dewdney
Manners Time by Elizabeth Verdick (Toddler Tools)
Mouse Says "Sorry" by Michael Dahl (Hello Genius)
The Nice Book by David Ezra Stein
No Hitting! by Karen Katz
Penguin Says "Please" by Michael Dahl (Hello Genius)
Please and Thank You! by Jill Ackerman (Little Scholastic)
Screen Time Is Not Forever by Elizabeth Verdick
Sharing by Yusuke Yonezu
Sharing Time by Elizabeth Verdick
Spot Says Please by Eric Hill
Teeth Are Not for Biting by Elizabeth Verdick
Thank You by Patricia Hegarty (Tiger Tales My Little World)
Uh-Oh! I'm Sorry by Jill Ackerman (Little Scholastic)
Words Are Not for Hurting by Elizabeth Verdick

	The Book You Chose	**Date Completed**
17.1 *Light Reader*		
17.2 *Interested Reader*		
17.3 *Avid Reader*		
17.4 *Committed Reader*		
17.5 *Enthralled Reader*		

Winter

Challenge 18

Babies in the Snow: First Lift-a-Flap by Ginger Swift
Baby Loves Winter! A Karen Katz Lift-the-Flap Book
Bear Snores On by Karma Wilson (The Bear Books)
Bears in the Snow by Shirley Parenteau
Bizzy Bear: Snow Sports by Benji Davies (Nosy Crow)
Bunny Slopes by Claudia Rueda
Colors in the Cold (Rookie Toddler)
The Colors of Winter by Danna Smith (Little Golden Book)
Curious George Curious about Winter by H. A. Rey
Daniel Plays in the Snow by Jason Fruchter (Daniel Tiger's Neighborhood)
Daniel's Winter Adventure by Jason Fruchter (Daniel Tiger's Neighborhood)
First Snow by Bomi Park
Good Night Ski Mountain by Adam Gamble
Good Night, Snow by Adam Gamble
Hooray for Snowy Days! by Susan Kantor
How to Build a Snowman by Jill Ackerman (Little Scholastic)
Ladybug Girl Ready for Snow by David Soman and Jacky Davis
Mouse's First Snow by Lauren Thompson

Penguin (DK Pop-Up Peekaboo)
Penguin and Pinecone by Salina Yoon
The Poky Little Puppy's Wonderful Winter Day by Jean Chandler (Little Golden Book)
Red Sled by Lita Judge
S is for Snow: A Snow ABC Primer by Ashley Marie Mireles
Snow by Jill McDonald (Hello, World)
Snow by Nancy Elizabeth Wallace
Snowflake Day! by Jason Fruchter (Daniel Tiger's Neighborhood)
The Snowy Day by Ezra Jack Keats
Ten Sparkly Snowflakes by Sean Julian (Tiger Tales)
Touch and Feel Winter (Scholastic Early Learners)
The Very Hungry Caterpillar's First Winter by Eric Carle
Walking in a Winter Wonderland illustrated by Tim Hopgood
Welcome Winter by Jill Ackerman (Little Scholastic)
Winter Babies by Kathryn O. Galbraith
Winter Dance by Marion Dane Bauer

	The Book You Chose	**Date Completed**
18.1 Light Reader		
18.2 Interested Reader		
18.3 Avid Reader		
18.4 Committed Reader		
18.5 Enthralled Reader		

Opposites

Challenge 19

Animal Opposites by Roger Priddy (Alphaprints)
Babies Love Opposites: Lift-a-Flap Book by Scarlett Wing
Baby Up Baby Down: A First Book of Opposites by Abrams Appleseed
Big and Little: A Book of Animal Opposites by Harriet Evans
Big and Little: A Book of Opposites by Carolina Buzio (Indestructibles)
Big and Little: Opposites Lift-a-Flap by Minnie Birdsong (Baby Einstein)
Big or Small? by Lenka Chytilova (First Words: Opposites)
Clifford's Opposites by Norman Bridwell (Clifford the Big Red Dog)
Crane Truck's Opposites by Sherri Duskey Rinker (Goodnight Goodnight Construction Site)
Eric Carle's Opposites
Hot Dog, Cold Dog (Rookie Toddler)
Jungle Gym by Jennifer Sattler
Kipper's Book of Opposites by Mick Inkpen
Learning with Llama Llama: Opposites by Anna Dewdney
Little Quack's Opposites by Lauren Thompson
London: A Book of Opposites by Ashley Evanson (Hello World)
My First Book of Opposites (Wonder House Books)
Oh My Oh My Oh Dinosaurs! A Book of Opposites by Sandra Boynton
Opposites (DK My First)
Opposites (Ladybird Baby Touch)
Opposites (Rookie Toddler)
Opposites by Agnese Baruzzi (Baby's First Library)
Opposites by Xavier Deneux (Touch Think Learn)
Opposites with Frank Lloyd Wright (Mudpuppy)
Sense and Sensibility adapted by Jennifer Adams (BabyLit)
Spot's Opposites by Eric Hill
Stop! Go! A Book of Opposites by Brian Biggs (Everything Goes)
Stop, Go, Yes, No! A Story of Opposites by Mike Twohy
Walk and See Opposites by Rosalind Beardshaw
What's Up, Duck? by Tad Hills (Duck and Goose)

	The Book You Chose	Date Completed
19.1 Light Reader		
19.2 Interested Reader		
19.3 Avid Reader		
19.4 Committed Reader		
19.5 Enthralled Reader		

Playtime

Challenge 20

Baby Peekaboo by Kate Merritt (Indestructibles)
Biscuit Loves the Park by Alyssa Satin Capucilli (I Can Read)
Bizzy Bear: Soccer Player by Benji Davies (Nosy Crow)
Busy Playtime (Campbell Books)
Busy Playtime by Rebecca Finn (Busy Books)
But Not the Hippopotamus by Sandra Boynton
Daniel and Max Play Together by Jason Fruchter (Daniel Tiger's Neighborhood)
Daniel Goes to the Playground by Becky Friedman (Daniel Tiger's Neighborhood)
Daniel Loves Playtime! by Alexandra Cassel Schwartz (Daniel Tiger's Neighborhood)
Dino-Mite Tag: A Lift-a-Flap Storybook by Morgan Huff
Join In and Play by Cheri J. Meiners (Learning to Get Along)
Ladybug Girl Plays by David Soman and Jacky Davis
Let's Play Football: Lift-a-Flap by Ginger Swift
Let's Play Soccer: Lift-a-Flap by Ginger Swift
Little Quack's Hide and Seek by Lauren Thompson
Llama Llama Time to Play: A Push-and-Pull Book by Anna Dewdney
Miffy Can Play! by R. J. Cregg (Ready to Read)
Nora's Ark by Eileen Spinelli
One Elephant Went Out to Play by Sanja Rescek (Child's Play)
Otis Loves to Play by Loren Long
Peekaboo (Ladybird Baby Touch)
Peekaboo Morning by Rachel Isadora
Peekaboo Rex! by Sandra Boynton
Play Ball! by Santiago Cohen
Playdate for Panda by Michael Dahl (Hello Genius)
Play Time for Puppy by Michael Dahl (Hello Genius)
Playtime (DK My First)
Playtime (DK Pop-Up Peekaboo)
Playtime Peekaboo! (DK)
Press Here by Herve Tullet
Sandbox by Rosemary Wells (Baby Max and Ruby)
Sign About Play Time by Anthony Lewis (Child's Play)
The Tickle Book by Heidi Kilgrass (Little Golden Book)
Tickle Me! (Ladybird Baby Touch)
Where Do Giggles Come From? by Diane E. Muldrow (Little Golden Book)
Who Says Peek a Boo? (Hightlights Baby Mirror Board Books)

	The Book You Chose	**Date Completed**
20.1 *Light Reader*		
20.2 *Interested Reader*		
20.3 *Avid Reader*		
20.4 *Committed Reader*		
20.5 *Enthralled Reader*		

Weather

Challenge 21

All About Weather: A First Weather Book for Kids by Huda Harajli
The Ants Go Marching by Dan Crisp (Child's Play)
Bear in Sunshine by Stella Blackstone
Find Spot on a Rainy Day: A Lift-the-Flap Book by Eric Hill
Hello, Weather! by Martha Day Zschock
I'm Sunny! by Jennifer L. Holm and Matthew Holm
In the Rain by Elizabeth Spurr
In the Snow by Elizabeth Spurr
In the Wind by Elizabeth Spurr
Itsy Bitsy Spider by Nora Hilb (Child's Play)
Kipper's Book of Weather by Mick Inkpen
Ladybug Girl and the Big Snow by David Soman and Jacky Davis
Little Cloud by Eric Carle
Little Raindrop (IglooBooks Nature Stories)
Little Snowflake by Suzanne Fossey
Our Weather by Jennifer Waddle (Little Hippo)
Peekaboo Sun by Camilla Reid (Nosy Crow)
Play in Any Weather by Lizzy Doyle (Indestructibles)
Rain! by Linda Ashman
Rain or Shine by Ronal Heuninck
Rain, Rain, Go Away by Caroline Jayne Church
Ready for Weather by Sarah Jones
Ruby and Rufus by Olivier Dunrea (Gossie and Friends)
Sunny or Cloudy? by Lenka Chytilova (First Words: Weather)
Weather by Anna Suessbauer (DK Spin and Spot)
Weather by Emmy Kastner (Nerdy Babies)
Weather by Jill McDonald (Hello, World)
Weather: Touch and Feel by Jessica Carapella (Little Hippo)
What Is the Weather Today? (Rookie Toddler)
The Wonder of Thunder by Sharon Purtill
Worm Weather by Jean Taft
Wuthering Heights: A BabyLit Weather Primer by Jennifer Adams

	The Book You Chose	**Date Completed**
21.1 *Light Reader*		
21.2 *Interested Reader*		
21.3 *Avid Reader*		
21.4 *Committed Reader*		
21.5 *Enthralled Reader*		

Shapes

Challenge 22

Apples and Robins by Lucie Felix
Baby, Find the Shapes by Ekaterina Trukhan (Indestructibles)
Big Box of Shapes by Wiley Blevins
Bulldozer's Shapes by Sherri Duskey Rinker (Goodnight Goodnight Construction Site)
Circle! Sphere! by Grace Lin (Storytelling Math)
Circus Shapes by Stuart J. Murphy (MathStarts)
City Shapes by Diana Murray
Corduroy's Shapes by MaryJo Scott
Do You See Shapes? (Rookie Toddler)
Learning with Llama Llama: Shapes by Anna Dewdney
Mouse Shapes by Ellen Stoll Walsh
My Favorite Book of Shapes by Erin Kelly (Rookie Toddler)
My First Book of Colors and Shapes (Rockridge Press)
My Turn to Learn Shapes by Natalie Marshall
My Very First Book of Shapes by Eric Carle
Our Favorite Shapes series by Beatrice Harris
Paris: A Book of Shapes by Ashley Evanson (Hello World)
Round Is a Tortilla: A Book of Shapes by Roseanne Thong
Shape Spotters by Megan E. Bryant (Penguin Young Readers)
Shape Up! Fun with Triangles and Other Polygons by David A. Adler
Shapes (DK My First)
Shapes! (National Geographic Kids)
Shapes in the Sky (Rookie Toddler)
Shapes: My First Pop-Up! by Matthew Reinhart
Shapes That Go (Rookie Toddler)
Snap: A Peek-Through Book of Shapes by Jonathan Litton (Tiger Tales: My Little World)
Spot's First Shapes by Eric Hill
Stanley's Shapes by William Bee
Tangled by Anne Miranda
Walter's Wonderful Web by Tim Hopgood

	The Book You Chose	**Date Completed**
22.1 Light Reader		
22.2 Interested Reader		
22.3 Avid Reader		
22.4 Committed Reader		
22.5 Enthralled Reader		

Love

Challenge 23

ABCs of Love by Patricia Hegarty
The ABCs of Love by Rose Rossner
Babies Love Valentines: Lift-a-Flap Book by Holly Berry-Byrd
Daniel Loves You by Alexandra Cassel (Daniel Tiger's Neighborhood)
Dinosaur, Dinosaur, I Love You and Other Rhymes by Sanja Rescek
Guess How Much I Love You by Sam McBratney
How Do I Love You? by Marion Dane Bauer
Hug Kiss Love: Lift-a-Flap by Scarlett Wing
If You Were Spaghetti by Haily and Kevin Meyers
I Love You (DK Baby Touch and Feel)
I Love You (DK Pop-Up Peekaboo)
I Love You As Big as the World by David Van Buren
I Love You Like No Otter by Rose Rossner (Punderland)
I Love You, Little One by Suzie Mason (Tiger Tales)
I Love You, Little Pookie by Sandra Boynton
I Love You More by Sierra Barela (Little Hippo)
I Love You More, Babysaur by Rose Rossner (Punderland)
I Love You Slow Much by Rose Rossner (Punderland)
I Love You, Spot by Eric Hall
I Love You Through and Through by Bernadette Rossetti-Shustak
Llama Llama I Love You by Anna Dewdney
Love You, Baby by Stephan Lomp (Indestructibles)
Love You Forever by Robert Munsch
Peekaboo Love by Camilla Reid (Nosy Crow)
Peek-a-Flap Love by Jaye Garnett (Cottage Door Press)
Pretty Loved by Mr. Jay
Somebunny Loves You by Rose Rossner (Punderland)
We Love Each Other by Yusuke Yonezu
What Does Baby Love? A Karen Katz Lift-the-Flap Book
Where Do Diggers Say I Love You? by Brianna Baplan Sayres
Who Says I Love You? (Highlights Baby Mirror Board Books)

	The Book You Chose	**Date Completed**
23.1 *Light Reader*		
23.2 *Interested Reader*		
23.3 *Avid Reader*		
23.4 *Committed Reader*		
23.5 *Enthralled Reader*		

Bathtime

Challenge 24

Bath Time by Eileen Spinelli
Bathtime (DK Baby Touch and Feel)
Bathtime for Biscuit by Alyssa Satin Capucilli (I Can Read)
Bears in the Bath by Shirley Parenteau
Brilliant Baby: It's Bath Time by Eva Remisova (Little Hippo)
Brush, Flush, Wash: Lift-a-Flap by Scarlett Wing
Daniel's Bath Time by Jason Fruchter (Daniel Tiger's Neighborhood)
Duck, Duck, Dinosaur: Bubble Blast by Kallie George (I Can Read)
Ella's Bathtime by Xenia Pavlova (Touch and Feel)
Five Little Monkeys Jump in the Bath by Eileen Christelow
Good Night Bath Time by Adam Gamble
Harry Takes a Bath by Harriet Ziefert (Penguin Young Readers)
How Do Bunnies Take Baths? by Diane Muldrow (Little Golden Book)
I Dig Bathtime by Brooke Jorden
I'm Not Taking a Bath by Laura Gehl (Peep and Egg)

It's Bath Time! by Carolina Buzio (Indestructibles)
Keep Squeaky Clean by Connie Whistler (Little Hippo)
Kid Tea by Elizabeth Ficocelli
Otter: Oh No, Bath Time! by Sam Garton (I Can Read)
Pig Takes a Bath by Michael Dahl (Hello Genius)
Puppy Mudge Takes a Bath by Cynthia Rylant (Ready-to-Read)
Rub-a-Dub-Dub by Page O'Rourke (So Tall Board Books)
Silly Monsters in the Bath by Pamela Chanko (Rookie Toddler)
Splish! Splash! (DK Baby Touch and Feel)
Splish, Splash, Baby! A Karen Katz Lift-the-Flap Book
Splish! Splash! Bathtime: Touch and Feel by Jennifer Schiavello (Little Hippo)

	The Book You Chose	**Date Completed**
24.1 Light Reader		
24.2 Interested Reader		
24.3 Avid Reader		
24.4 Committed Reader		
24.5 Enthralled Reader		

Birthdays

Challenge 25

Bears and a Birthday by Shirley Parenteau (Bears on Chairs)
Bear's Birthday by Stella Blackstone
Birthday by Rosemary Wells (Baby Max and Ruby)
The Birthday Box by Leslie Patricelli
A Birthday for Cow! by Jan Thomas (The Giggle Gang)
Birthday Monsters! by Sandra Boynton
Biscuit's Birthday by Alyssa Satin Capucilli
Bunny Party by Rosemary Wells (Max and Ruby)
Find and Point Birthday by Marisa Wallin (Rookie Toddler)
Happy Birthday (DK Baby Touch and Feel)
Happy Birthday! (Ladybird Baby Touch)
Happy Birthday: Touch and Feel by Jennifer Schiavello
Happy Birthday by Yu-hsuan Huang (Sing Along with Me)
Happy Birthday, Curious George by H.A. Rey
Happy Birthday from the Very Hungry Caterpillar by Eric Carle
Happy Birthday, Little Pookie by Sandra Boynton
Happy Birthday, Sophie! (DK Sophie La Girafe)
It's My Birthday by Helen Oxenbury
Kipper's Birthday by Mick Inkpen
Max's Birthday by Rosemary Wells (Max and Ruby)
Now I Am 1: A Collection of Rhymes to Share by Rachel Baines
Spot's Birthday Party by Eric Hill
The Very Hungry Caterpillar's Birthday Party by Eric Carle
Where Is Baby's Birthday Cake? A Lift-the-Flap Book by Karen Katz
You're One! by Shelly Unwin
You're Two! by Shelly Unwin

	The Book You Chose	**Date Completed**
25.1 Light Reader		
25.2 Interested Reader		
25.3 Avid Reader		
25.4 Committed Reader		
25.5 Enthralled Reader		

Spring

Challenge 26

- *Baby Loves Spring! A Karen Katz Lift-the-Flap Book*
- *Bear Wants More* by Karma Wilson (The Bear Books)
- *The Book of Spring* by Agnese Baruzzi
- *Five Little Ducks* by Yu-hsuan Huang (Sing Along with Me)
- *Guess What? – Flowers* by Yusuke Yonezu
- *Here Comes Spring!* by Susan Kantor
- *In My Flower* by Sara Gillingham
- *In My Meadow* by Sara Gillingham
- *I See Spring* by Charles Ghigna
- *Little Blue Truck's Springtime: A Lift-the-Flap Book* by Alice Schertle
- *A Little Book About Spring* (Leo Lionni's Friends)
- *Mrs. Peaknuckle's Flower Alphabet*
- *Night Night, Bunny* by Amy Parker
- *Peekaboo Chick* by Camilla Reid (Nosy Crow)
- *The Poky Little Puppy's Special Spring Day* by Diane Muldrow (Little Golden Book)
- *Red Hat* by Lita Judge
- *Sleeping Bunnies* by Yu-hsuan Huang (Sing Along with Me)
- *Spring* by Chris Demarest
- *Spring* by Gerda Muller
- *Spring Is Here* by Lois Lenski
- *A Spring Surprise: A Peter Rabbit Tale* by Beatrix Potter
- *The Very Hungry Caterpillar's First Spring* by Eric Carle
- *Welcome Spring* by Jill Ackerman (Little Scholastic)
- *What Is Spring?* by Sonali Fry
- *You Are My Baby: Meadow* by Lorena Siminovich

	The Book You Chose	**Date Completed**
26.1 *Light Reader*		
26.2 *Interested Reader*		
26.3 *Avid Reader*		
26.4 *Committed Reader*		
26.5 *Enthralled Reader*		

Backyard

Challenge 27

Baby's First Book of Birds and Colors by Phyllis Limbacher Tildes
Backyard (Usborne Look and Say)
Backyard All Year: Touch and Feel by Minnie Birdsong (Baby Einstein)
Backyard Birds: A Numbers Book by Chloe Goodhart (Birding for Babies)
Backyard Bugs by Jill McDonald (Hello, World!)
Backyard Bugs: Touch and Feel by Terry Baddoo
Big Backyard: Summer, Fall, Winter & Spring! by Redd Byrd
Biscuit in the Garden by Alyssa Satin Capucilli (I Can Read)
Biscuit Wants to Play by Alyssa Satin Capucilli (I Can Read)
Busy Garden by Rebecca Finn (Busy Books)
Garden by Anna Milbourne (Usborne Little Lift and Look)
Garden Days with Bumblebee by Ryan Barone (Little Hippo)
Garden Time by Jill McDonald (Hello, World)
I Spy Backyard Bugs! by Raphael Dali
Inside Outside by Lizi Boyd
Let's Go Outside! by Ekaterina Trukhan (Indestructibles)
Little Acorn (Nature Stories)
Memory Match in the Garden: Lift-the-Flap Book by Anne Paradis
Mrs. Peaknuckle's Tree Alphabet
My First Book of Flowers (Wonder House Books)
My Little Garden by Katrin Wiehle
Tap the Magic Tree by Christie Matheson
Who Is in the Garden? by Simon Abbott
Who's Hiding in the Garden? A Lift-the-Flap Book by Amelia Hepworth
You Are My Baby: Garden by Lorena Siminovich

	The Book You Chose	**Date Completed**
27.1 Light Reader		
27.2 Interested Reader		
27.3 Avid Reader		
27.4 Committed Reader		
27.5 Enthralled Reader		

Pets

Challenge 28

Adorable Pets: Touch and Feel by Anna Jones (Little Hippo)
Babies Love Kittens: Lift-a-Flap Book by Scarlett Wing
Babies Love Puppies: Lift-a-Flap Book by Scarlett Wing
Baby's First Pets by Scott Barker (Little Hippo)
Biscuit Feeds the Pets by Alyssa Satin Capucilli (I Can Read)
Biscuit Meets the Class Pet by Alyssa Satin Capucilli (I Can Read)
Bunny (DK Baby Touch and Feel)
Busy Pets by Louise Forshaw (Busy Books)
Happy and Honey by Laura Godwin (Ready to Read)
Hello, Puppy by Parragon Books
I Love Puppies by Amanda Miller (Rookie Toddler)
I'm Thinking of a Pet by Guillain and Gaggiotti (Nosy Crow)
Kitten (DK Baby Touch and Feel)
Let's Find the Kitten (Tiger Tales)
Let's Find the Puppy (Tiger Tales)
Mittens, Where Is Max? by Lola M. Schaefer (I Can Read)
My Favorite Pets by Jill Ackerman (Little Scholastic)
My First Touch and Feel Pets (Tiger Tales)
My Pets by Margaret O'Hair (Board Buddies)
Otter: What Pet Is Best? by Sam Garton (I Can Read)
Peekaboo Pets by Sydnie Wittenberg (Little Hippo)
Perfect Pets by Roger Priddy (Bright Baby Touch and Feel)
Pet Families (Poke-a-Dot)
A Pet for Pete by James Dean (I Can Read)
Pets (Ladybird Baby Touch)
Pets by Jill McDonald (Hello, World)
Puppies and Kittens (DK Baby Touch and Feel)
Puppies and Kittens: Touch and Feel by Jennifer Schiavello
Puppy (DK Baby Touch and Feel)
Where Is Baby's Puppy? A Karen Katz Lift-the-Flap Book
You Are My Baby: Pets by Lorena Siminovich

	The Book You Chose	**Date Completed**
28.1 *Light Reader*		
28.2 *Interested Reader*		
28.3 *Avid Reader*		
28.4 *Committed Reader*		
28.5 *Enthralled Reader*		

Numbers

Challenge 29

123 (DK Baby Touch and Feel)
123 (DK My First)
123 by Tad Hills (Duck and Goose)
123 Beep Beep Beep: A Counting Book by Brian Biggs (Everything Goes)
1 Is One by Tasha Tudor
Babies Love Numbers by Scarlett Wing
Baby, Let's Count! by Ekaterina Trukkan (Indestructibles)
Baby's 123: A Counting Song by Art Seiden (So Tall Board Books)
Bear Counts by Karma Wilson (The Bear Books)
Click, Clack, Splish, Splash: A Counting Adventure by Doreen Cronin
Corduroy's Numbers by MaryJo Scott
Countablock by Christopher Franceschelli
Counting (DK Baby Touch and Feel)
Counting Cars and Trucks (Rookie Toddler)
Counting Kisses by Karen Katz
Counting Tools 1 to 10 (Scholastic)
Doggies: A Counting and Barking Book by Sandra Boynton
Excavator's 123 by Sherri Duskey Rinker (Goodnight Goodnight Construction Site)
Fifteen Animals! by Sandra Boynton
First 100 Numbers by Roger Priddy
Flamingo: A Playful Book of Counting by Patricia Hegarty (Tiger Tales: My Little World)
Hide 'n' Sheep by Jennifer Sattler
Hoot: A Hide-and-Seek Book of Counting by Jonathan Litton (Tiger Tales: My Little World)
I Have a Secret: A First Counting Book by Carl Memling
Is That Wise, Pig? by Jan Thomas
Jungle Counting by Scott Barker (Little Hippo)
Kipper's Book of Numbers by Mick Inkpen
The Last Marshmallow by Grace Lin
Learning with Llama Llama: Numbers by Anna Dewdney
Little Buckaroo and Lou by Jennifer Sattler
Little Quack Counts by Lauren Thompson
Monsters Play...Counting! by Flavia Z. Drago
More or Less (Rookie Toddler)
My Favorite Book of Numbers (Rookie Toddler)
My First Book of Numbers (Wonder House Books)
My First Counting Book by Lilian Moore (Little Golden Book)
Numbers (DK Pop-Up Peekaboo)
Numbers by Xavier Deneux (Touch Think Learn)
Numbers by Roger Priddy (Bright Baby)
One Boy by Laura Vaccaro Seeger
One Ted Falls Out of Bed: A Counting Story by Julia Donaldson
One, Two, Buckle My Shoes by Salina Yoon
One, Two, Three! A Happy Counting Book by Sandra Boynton
Poppy and Sam's Counting Book by Sam Taplin (Usborne)
Richard Scarry's Best Counting Book by Richard Scarry
Romeo & Juliet: A BabyLit Counting Primer by Jennifer Adams
Rooster's Off to See the World by Eric Carle
San Francisco by Ashley Evanson (Hello World)
Seek and Count by Yusuke Yonezu
See, Touch, Feel 123 by Roger Priddy
Splish, Splash, Splosh by David Melling
Spot Can Count by Eric Hill
Walk and See 123 by Rosalind Beardshaw (Nosy Crow)

	The Book You Chose	**Date Completed**
29.1 *Light Reader*		
29.2 *Interested Reader*		
29.3 *Avid Reader*		
29.4 *Committed Reader*		
29.5 *Enthralled Reader*		

Feelings
Challenge 30

Babies Love Kindness: Lift-a-Flap Book by Ginger Swift
Baby's Feelings: A First Book of Emotions by Kayla McGrath
Bear Feels Scared by Karma Wilson (The Bear Books)
The Boy and the Bear by Peter Stein
Calm-Down Time by Elizabeth Verdick (Toddler Tools)
Can You Make a Happy Face? by Janice Behrens
Chester the Brave by Audrey Penn (The Kissing Hand)
Daniel Feels Left Out by Maggie Testa (Daniel Tiger's Neighborhood)
Daniel Feels One Stripe Nervous by Jason Fruchter (Daniel Tiger's Neighborhood)
Daniel Gets Scared by Maggie Testa (Daniel Tiger's Neighborhood)
Daniel Misses Someone by Jason Fruchter (Daniel Tiger's Neighborhood)
Dogger by Shirley Hughes
Duck and Goose: How Are You Feeling? by Tad Hills
Emma: An Emotions Primer by Jennifer Adams (BabyLit)
Feelings (Ladybird Baby Touch)
Feelings by Xavier Deneux (Touch Think Learn)
Happy Hippo, Angry Duck by Sandra Boynton
How Does Baby Feel? A Karen Katz Lift-the-Flap Book
How Do You Feel by Jodie Shepherd (Rookie Toddler)
How Is Daniel Feeling? by Maggie Testa (Daniel Tiger's Neighborhood)

I Love It When You Smile by Sam McBratney
I'm Feeling Happy by Natalie Shaw (Daniel Tiger's Neighborhood)
I'm Feeling Mad by Natalie Shaw (Daniel Tiger's Neighborhood)
I'm Feeling Sad by Natalie Shaw (Daniel Tiger's Neighborhood)
I'm Feeling Silly by Natalie Shaw (Daniel Tiger's Neighborhood)
I'm Feeling Thankful by Natalie Shaw (Daniel Tiger's Neighborhood)
I'm Grumpy by Jennifer L. Holm and Matthew Holm
I'm Scared by Jennifer L. Holm and Matthew Holm
I'm Sunny by Jennifer L. Holm (My First Comics)
The Kissing Hand by Audrey Penn
Little Monkey Calms Down by Michael Dahl
Llama Llama Mad at Mama by Anna Dewdney
Llama Llama Misses Mama by Anna Dewdney
Making Faces: A First Book of Emotions by Abrams Appleseed
Mama Travels for Work by Jason Fruchter (Daniel Tiger's Neighborhood)
Moody Monsters by Chloe Marie (Little Hippo)
My Friend Is Sad by Mo Willems
No Worries for Whale by Michael Dahl (Hello Genius)

Ollie's Hug by Olivier Dunrea (Gossie and Friends)
Penguin Misses Mom by Michael Dahl (Hello Genius)
The Pigeon Has Feelings, Too by Mo Willems
The Poky Little Puppy and the Patchword Blanket by Jean Chandler (Little Golden Book)
The Pout-Pout Fish by Deborah Diesen
Quick as a Cricket by Audrey Wood
Remembering Blue Fish by Jason Fruchter (Daniel Tiger's Neighborhood)
Tickle Time! by Sandra Boynton
What's Wrong, Little Pookie? by Sandra Boynton
Who Is Smiling? by Yusuke Yonezu
A Whole Bunch of Feelings by Jennifer Moore-Mallinos
Why Cry? By Yusuke Yonezu
Worries Are Not Forever by Elizabeth Verdick (Best Behavior Series)

	The Book You Chose	**Date Completed**
30.1 *Light Reader*		
30.2 *Interested Reader*		
30.3 *Avid Reader*		
30.4 *Committed Reader*		
30.5 *Enthralled Reader*		

Toys
Challenge 31

Ball by John Hutton
Ball by Mary Sullivan
A Ball for Daisy by Chris Raschka
Biscuit and the Lost Teddy Bear by Alyssa Satin Capucilli (I Can Read)
Corduroy by Don Freeman
Corduroy's Toys by Don Freeman
I Like Toys! by Lorena Siminovich
Kipper's Beach Ball by Mick Inkpen
Kipper's Toybox by Mick Inkpen
Kitten (DK Pop-Up Peekaboo)
Max's Toys by Rosemary Wells (Max and Ruby)
Mr. Noah and His Family by Jane Werner (Little Golden Book)
My First Book of Toys (Wonder House Books)
My First Toys (IglooBooks)
Noisy Toys Peekaboo! (DK)
A Pocket for Corduroy by Don Freeman
Puppies (DK Pop-Up Peekaboo)
Stanley's Toy Box by William Bee
Teddy Bear, Teddy Bear and Other Favorite Nursery Rhymes by Steven Lenton (Tiger Tales)
Teddy Bear, Teddy Bear, Turn Around! (Rookie Toddler)
Touch and Feel Toys (DK)
Touch and Feel Toys by Jessica Carapella (Little Hippo)
Toy Boat by Randall de Seve
Toys: A Black-and-White Book (Baby Touch)
Watch Me Throw the Ball by Mo Willems

	The Book You Chose	**Date Completed**
31.1 *Light Reader*		
31.2 *Interested Reader*		
31.3 *Avid Reader*		
31.4 *Committed Reader*		
31.5 *Enthralled Reader*		

Space

Challenge 32

A Is for Astronaut: An Out-of-This-World Alphabet Adventure by Jennifer Levasseur (Smithsonian Kids)
Astronauts by Christiane Engel (First Explorers)
Astronomy by Alex Fabrizio (Baby's Big World)
Babies Love Outer Space by Susanne König
Baby Astronaut by Laura Gehl (Baby Scientist)
Baby Loves Aerospace Engineering! by Ruth Spiro
Bizzy Bear: Space Rocket by Benji Davies (Nosy Crow)
Future Astronaut by Lori Alexander (Future Baby)
Good Night Astronauts by Adam Gamble
Good Night, Galaxy by Adam Gamble
Good Night Solar System by Adam Gamble
I Love Space by Allison Wortche and Steve Mack
Look, There's a Rocket! by Esther Aarts (Nosy Crow)
Moon and Stars by Anna Suessbauer (Spin and Spot)
Moon Landing by Jill McDonald (Hello, World)
My Best Pop-up Space Book (DK)
Our Solar System: Touch and Feel by Jennifer Waddle
Outer Space: Touch and Feel by Jessica Carapella (Little Hippo)
Roaring Rockets by Tony Mitton and Ant Parker (Amazing Machines)
Rocket by Amelia Hepworth (How It Works)
Rocket Science by Alex Fabrizo (Baby's Big World)
S is for Space: A Space ABC Primer by Ashley Marie Mireles
Solar System by Jill McDonald (Hello, World)
Space (DK Pop-Up Peekaboo)
Space by Emmy Kastner (Nerdy Babies)
Space by John Townsend
Stars! Stars! Stars! by Nancy Elizabeth Wallace
To the Moon: A Push-and-Pull Adventure (Little World)
Twinkle, Twinkle, Little Star by Iza Trapani
Twinkle, Twinkle, Little Star by Joe Rhatigan (Little Hippo)
Where's the Astronaut? by Ingela P. Arrhenius (Nosy Crow)

	The Book You Chose	**Date Completed**
32.1 *Light Reader*		
32.2 *Interested Reader*		
32.3 *Avid Reader*		
32.4 *Committed Reader*		
32.5 *Enthralled Reader*		

Bedtime
Challenge 33

Baby Night-Night by Kate Merritt (Indestructibles)
Baby's First Bedtime by Scott Barker (Little Hippo)
Bear Can't Sleep by Karma Wilson (The Bear Books)
Bears in Beds by Shirley Parenteau (Bears on Chairs)
Bedtime by Elizabeth Verdick (Toddler Tools)
Bedtime Baby by Genine Delahaye (Tiger Tales)
A Bedtime for Bear by Bonny Becker (Bear and Mouse)
Bedtime in the Meadow by Stephanie Shaw
Beep! Beep! Go to Sleep! by Todd Tarpley
Biscuit by Alyssa Satin Capucilli
Brownie & Pearl Hit the Hay by Cynthia Rylant
Clifford's Bedtime by Norman Bridwell
Daniel's First Sleepover by Angela C. Santomero (Daniel Tiger's Neighborhood)
Dinosaur, Dinosaur, Say Good Night and Other Bedtime Rhymes illustrated by Sanja Rescek (Tiger Tales)
Dinosnores by Sandra Boynton
Find It: Bedtime (Highlights)
The Going to Bed Book by Sandra Boynton
Good Night, Adventure Bay! (Paw Patrol)
Good Night, Animals (Poke-a-Dot)
Good Night, Curious George by Margaret and H.A. Rey
Good Night, I Love You by Caroline Jane Church
Good Night, Little Blue Truck by Alice Schertle
Good Night, Octopus by Caleb Burroughs (I Can Do It)
Goodnight, Daniel Tiger by Angela C. Santomero
Goodnight Everyone by Chris Haughton
Goodnight Moon by Margaret Wise Brown
Goodnight, Sophie (DK Sophie La Girafe)
Grab Your Pillow, Armadillo by Haily and Kevin Meyers
How Do You Sleep? by Louise Bonnett-Rampersaud
Hush! A Thai Lullaby by Minfong
Hush, Little Baby by Marla Frazee

If Animals Kissed Good Night by Ann Whitford Paul
I'm Not Tired! A Bedtime Routine Book by Janice Behrens
It's Bedtime by Sandra Magsamen (Looky Looky Little One)
Ladybug Girl Says Good Night by David Soman and Jacky Davis
Little Quack's Bedtime by Lauren Thompson
Llama Llama Nighty-Night by Anna Dewdney
A Lullaby for Little One by Dawn Casey
Max's Bedtime by Rosemary Wells (Max and Ruby)
My Bed: Enchanting Ways to Fall Asleep Around the World by Rebecca Bond
My Favorite Bedtime Rhymes (Tiger Tales)
Night! Night! Bedtime by Jennifer Schiavello
Night-Night (Ladybird Baby Touch)
Night-Night, Little Pookie by Sandra Boynton
Pajama Time! by Sandra Boynton
Peekaboo Moon by Camilla Reid (Nosy Crow)
Poppy and Sam's Bedtime Stories by Heather Amery and Lesley Sims (Usborne)
Princess Baby, Night-Night by Karen Katz
Put on Your PJs, Piggies by Laura Neutzling
Rabbit's Bedtime by Nancy Elizabeth Wallace
Richard Scarry's Bedtime Stories by Richard Scarry
Richard Scarry's Good Night, Little Bear by Patsy Scarry (Little Golden Book)
Rocket-Bye Baby: A Spaceflight Lullaby by Danna Smith (Little Golden Book)
Silly Lullaby by Sandra Boynton
Sleepy Time by Gyo Fujikawa
Spot Loves Bedtime by Eric Hill
Ten, Nine, Eight by Molly Bang
Time for Bed by Vicki L. Weber
Time for Bed, Nori by Brigitte Weninger

	The Book You Chose	**Date Completed**
33.1 *Light Reader*		
33.2 *Interested Reader*		
33.3 *Avid Reader*		
33.4 *Committed Reader*		
33.5 *Enthralled Reader*		

Mommies & Daddies

Challenge 34

ABCs of Love for Mom by Patricia Hegarty
Baby Penguins Love Their Mama by Melissa Guion
Busy Daddy by Louise Forshaw (Busy Books)
Daddies by Janet Frank (Little Golden Book)
Daddy and Me by Tiya Hall and Sydney Hanson
Daddy and Me: A Lift-the-Flap Book by Karen Katz
Daddy Hugs by Karen Katz
Daddy Loves Me 1, 2, 3 by Toni Armier (Little Hippo)
Good Night, Daddy by Adam Gamble
Good Night Mommy by Adam Gamble
Hello Daddy! (Ladybird Touch and Feel)
Hello, Mommy! (Ladybird Touch and Feel)
I Love Dad with the Very Hungry Caterpillar by Eric Carle
I Love Mom with the Very Hungry Caterpillar by Eric Carle
I Love My Daddy by Giles Andreae
I Love My Daddy Because... by Laurel Porter Gaylord
I Love My Mommy by Giles Andreae
I Love My Mommy Because... by Laurel Porter Gaylord
I Love My Mummy (Campbell Books)
I Love You, Dad by Jason Fruchter (Daniel Tiger's Neighborhood)
I Love You, Daddy. by Edie Evans (Little Golden Book)
I Love You, Daddy by Jilliam Harker
I Love You, Daddy by Brooke Vitale (Little Hippo)
I Love You, Mom by Jason Fruchter (Daniel Tiger's Neighborhood)
I Love You, Mommy by Edie Evans (Little Golden Book)
I Love You, Mommy by Jilliam Harker
I Love You, Mommy by Brooke Vitale (Little Hippo)
Just Like My Papa by Toni Buzzeo
Ladybug Girl and Her Mama by David Soman and Jacky Davis
Ladybug Girl and Her Papa by David Soman and Jacky Davis
Mama Always Comes Home by Karma Wilson
Mama, Do You Love Me? by Barbara M. Joose
Mama Saurus by Stephan Lomp
Me and My Dad! by Alison Ritchie
Me and My Mom! by Alison Ritchie
Mommy and Me by Tiya Hall and Sydney Hanson
Mommy Hugs by Karen Katz
Mommy Loves Me 1, 2, 3 by Toni Armier (Little Hippo)
Mommy, Where Are You? A Lift-a-Flap Storybook by Morgan Huff
My Dad Loves Me! by Marianne Richmond
My Mom Loves Me! by Marianne Richmond
Night Night, Daddy by Amy Parker
Night Night, Mommy by Amy Parker
Papa Saurus by Stephan Lomp
Spot Loves His Daddy by Eric Hill
Spot Loves His Mommy by Eric Hill
That's My Daddy! by Ann Hodgman
That's My Mommy! by Ann Hodgman
Where Is Baby's Mommy? by Karen Katz

	The Book You Chose	**Date Completed**
34.1 Light Reader		
34.2 Interested Reader		
34.3 Avid Reader		
34.4 Committed Reader		
34.5 Enthralled Reader		

Ocean

Challenge 35

All Around the Sea (Poke-a-Dot)
Babies in the Ocean: First Lift-a-Flap by Ginger Swift
Baby's First Ocean by Scott Barker (Little Hippo)
Bizzy Bear: Deep-Sea Diver by Benji Davies (Nosy Crow)
Black and White Ocean by Charles Reasoner
Colorful Ocean Adventure: Pop Tales (Little Hippo)
Exploring Sharks by Jill McDonald (Hello, World)
Good Night Coral Reef by Adam Gamble
Good Night Ocean by Mark Jasper
Hello, Ocean! by Martha Zschock
Hello, Ocean Friends! by Lila Mitzie (Little Hippo)
I'm Thinking of an Ocean Animal by Guillain and Gaggiotti
In the Ocean by Neil Clark
In the Ocean: Peek and Seek by Sarah Muthomi
Little Fish's Ocean by Lucy Cousins
Silly Sea Creatures by Connie Whistler (Little Hippo)
Memory Match Under the Sea by Anne Paradis
Mrs. Peanuckle's Ocean Alphabet
My Little Ocean by Katrin Wiehle
O Is for Ocean by Greg Paprocki
Ocean by Jean Claude (DK Pop-Up Peekaboo)
Ocean by Emmy Kastner (Nerdy Babies)
Ocean Days with Crab by Ryan Barone (Little Hippo)
Ocean Friends: Touch and Feel by Jennifer Schiavello
Ocean Life by Jill McDonald (Hello, World)
Peekaboo! in the Ocean by Cocoretto
Peekaboo Ocean by Sydnie Wittenberg (Little Hippo)
Sea Creatures (First Explorers)
Silly Sea Creatures (Little Hippo)
Sparkle-Go-Seek Ocean: Lift-the-Flap by Bethany Carr
Ten Splishy, Splashy Fish: Colorful Countdown Fun! by Debbie Tarbett (Tiger Tales)
Under the Sea (DK Pop-Up Peekaboo)
Under the Sea by Ryan Barone (Little Hippo)
Under the Sea by Sandra Magsamen (Looky Looky Little One)
Under the Sea by Anna Milbourne (Usborne Little Lift and Look)
We Are Friends Under the Sea by Sue Downing (DK)
Who Is in the Ocean? by Simon Abbott
Who's in the Ocean? (Poke-a-Dot)

	The Book You Chose	**Date Completed**
35.1 *Light Reader*		
35.2 *Interested Reader*		
35.3 *Avid Reader*		
35.4 *Committed Reader*		
35.5 *Enthralled Reader*		

Summer
Challenge 36

Baby Loves Summer! A Karen Katz Lift-the-Flap Book
Beach Baby by Kate Merritt (Indestructibles)
Beach Day! by Anahid Hamparian
Better Not Get Wet, Jesse Bear by Nancy White Carlstrom
Brownie and Pearl Take a Dip by Cynthia Rylant
Busy Beach (Campbell Books)
Busy Swimming (Campbell Books)
The Colors of Summer by Danna Smith (Little Golden Book)
Curious George Curious about Summer by H.A. Rey
Curious George Goes Swimming by Margret and H.A. Rey
Good Night, Beach by Adam Gamble
Good Night, Summer by Adam Gamble
Hooray for Sunny Days! by Susan Kantor
I See Summer by Charles Ghigna
Llama Llama Sand and Sun by Anna Dewdney
Lois Looks for Bob at the Beach by Gerry Turley
Mama, Is It Summer Yet? by Nikki McClure
Mouse's First Summer by Lauren Thompson
On My Beach by Sara Gillingham
Summer by Gerda Muller
Swim! by Marilyn Brigham (Board Buddies)
The Very Hungry Caterpillar's First Summer by Eric Carle
Welcome Summer by Jill Ackerman (Little Scholastic)
Where Is Baby's Beach Ball? A Lift-the-Flap Book by Karen Katz
Who's Hiding at the Beach? by Katharine McEwen (Nosy Crow)

	The Book You Chose	**Date Completed**
36.1 *Light Reader*		
36.2 *Interested Reader*		
36.3 *Avid Reader*		
36.4 *Committed Reader*		
36.5 *Enthralled Reader*		

Book Awards & Party

Do This As Soon As You Finish Your Reading Challenge

Grab your child's completed reading log and help him fill out the awards page (opposite page) to give his best and worst books an official award and mark them as most memorable this year.

Encourage him not to agonize over "was this one really the best…" but to go with his general impressions or write down all the contenders.

Send us a copy of this at books@timberdoodle.com, and we'll be thrilled to credit you 50 Doodle Dollar reward points (worth $2.50 off your next order) as our thank-you for taking the time to share. We'll also congratulate your child on a job so well done!

Bonus Idea

Have an awards ceremony night all about one of the books on your list! You'll get the most specific ideas by searching online for "book I picked theme party," but here are some things to think through as you get started.

Food: how can you tie the menu to the theme? A book like *Green Eggs and Ham* or *Pancakes for Breakfast* is easy—just replicate the food in the book! If you're working with a book that doesn't feature food directly, there are a few options. Perhaps the book featured a construction crew; you could all eat from "lunchboxes" tonight or set up your kitchen to masquerade as a food truck. Or if you're reading a book about the pioneers, do a little research and eat frying pan bread, beans, venison, and cornmeal mush.

You could also take the food you would normally eat and reshape it to match your story. For instance, sandwiches can be cut into ships, round apple slices can be life preservers, crackers can be labeled "hardtack," and you're well on your way to a party featuring your favorite nautical tale.

Don't forget the setting. As ridiculous as it sounds, eating dinner by (battery-operated!) lantern light under your table draped with blankets will make that simple camping tale an experience your family will be recalling for years to come.

Or perhaps some handmade red table fans, softly playing traditional Chinese music, and a red tablecloth would provide the perfect backdrop for the story about life in China.

The more senses you use, the more memorable you make this experience. Use appropriate background music, diffuse peppermint oil to make it smell like Christmas, dim the lights, eat at the top of the swing set, or whatever would set this apart from a regular night and make it just a bit more interesting.

Don't get trapped in either the "we must do this tonight" mode or the "we can't do this because it won't be perfect" mode. Allowing your child to spend a few days creating decorations and menus is wonderful! Doing it today because it's the only free night on the horizon even though you can only integrate a few ideas into the preset menu? Also amazing! Your goal is to value the book and make some fun memories.

Timberdoodle.com | 800-478-0672

Book Awards of

_____
(Your Child's Name Here)   (Year Here)

I Read _____ Books From The Reading Challenge This Year!

Funniest Book:
_____

Most Memorable Book:
_____

Book I Read The Most Times:
_____

Book I Enjoyed The Least:
_____

Teacher's Favorite Book:
_____

Book I Most Wish Was A Series:
_____

Choose Your Own Award:
_____

When You're Done Here

Your Top 4 FAQ about Next Year

Things to Think through as You Anticipate Preschool

So you're finishing up Tiny Tots already? How has it gone for you? Really, we'd love to know! (Plus, you get reward points for your review.) Just jump over to the Tiny Tots Curriculum page on our website and scroll down to submit a review.

As you look toward next year, there are a few things that you may want to know.

1. When Can We See the New Kits?

New kits usually release in April. Check our Facebook page or give us a call for this year's projection, but it's always in the spring and usually mid-April.

2. Free Customization

If your child has raced ahead in some subjects this year, or if you need to go back and fill in some gaps, or if you don't need more Math-U-See blocks, you'll be thrilled to know that you can customize your kit next year. You'll find full details on our website, but know that customization is free and can often be completed online if you prefer to DIY.

3. Do I Need to Take the Summer Off?

Some students finish a grade with an eager passion to jump right into the next grade, and parents contact us asking if that's OK or if they should take some time off so the child doesn't burn out. We are year-round homeschoolers, so we would definitely be fans of jumping into the next grade!

However, the truth is that this is your decision. We can tell you that a long break can quench the thirst for knowledge, and that's why our family typically moves right into the next grade. However, sometimes a little suspense makes the year begin with beautiful anticipation. If you have a crazy summer planned, it can be ideal to set school aside and enjoy the season!

If you decide to start early, you could consider saving 1 or 2 items for your official start date so that there is still some anticipation.

4. Can I Refill This Kit for My Next Child?

Absolutely! Each year's Additional Student Kit reflects the current year's kit (so the 2024-2025 Elite Curriculum Kit and the 2024-2025 Additional Student Kit correlate). If you loved it just the way it was, refill it now before we swap things around for next year. Or, if you prefer, wait for the new kits to launch and then let our team help you figure out what tweaks (if any) need to be made.

We're Here to Help!

If you have other questions for us, want to share additional feedback, or would like to get in touch for some other reason, don't hesitate to drop us a line or give us a call. (FYI, we also have online chat on our website if that's easier for you.)

mail@Timberdoodle.com
800-478-0672

Doodle Dollar Reward Points

What They Are, How They Work, and Where to Find Them

If you're one of our Charter School BFFs, we just want to give you a heads up that the following information doesn't really apply to you. Doodle Dollars are earned on individual prepaid orders (credit cards or online payment plans are fine) and sadly don't apply to purchase orders or school district orders.

Now, with that out of the way, here's the good news. Almost any item you order directly from us earns you reward points!

You will earn 1 point for every $1 you spend.
20 points = $1 off a future order!

Some families prefer to use this money as they go, while others save it up for Christmas or for those midyear purchases that just weren't in the budget.

Can I Earn More Points?

Absolutely! Review your purchases on Timberdoodle.com to earn points. Add pictures for even more points!

What Can I Spend My Points On?

Anything on our website. These reward points act as a gift certificate to be used on anything you like.

How Do I Get to My Points?

The simplest way is to look for the teal Doodle Dollars pop-up in the lower left corner of our website. Click it, log in, then click "All Rewards" > "Redeem" and drag the slider to choose how many points to cash out. You'll immediately be issued a gift certificate to apply to your order. If you run into any challenges, please let our team know, and we will be thrilled to assist you.

Check our website for the latest information on reward points:
www.Timberdoodle.com/doodledollars

Photo: The Browns in Miami, Florida

Printed in the USA
CPSIA information can be obtained
at www.ICGtesting.com
CBHW081210250724
11954CB00003B/11